START & RUN A
SECURITY BUSINESS

START & RUN A
SECURITY BUSINESS

Katherine Matak

Self-Counsel Press
(a division of)
International Self-Counsel Press Ltd.
USA   Canada

Self-Counsel Press acknowledges the financial support of the Government of Canada through the Canada Book Fund (CBF) for our publishing activities.

Printed in Canada.

First edition: 2016

Library and Archives Canada Cataloguing in Publication

Matak, Katherine, author
    Start & run a security business / Katherine Matak.

(Start & run)
Issued in print and electronic formats.
ISBN 978-1-77040-246-1 (paperback).—ISBN 978-1-77040-452-6 (epub).—ISBN 978-1-77040-453-3 (kindle)
    1. Private security services--Canada—Management. 2. New business enterprises--Canada. I. Title. II. Title: Start and run a security business.

HV8291.C3M38 2015	658.4'70971	C2015-905107-X
		C2015-905108-8

Self-Counsel Press
(a division of)
International Self-Counsel Press Ltd.

Bellingham, WA
USA

North Vancouver, BC
Canada

CONTENTS

NOTICE TO READERS

ACKNOWLEDGMENTS

I would like to dedicate this book to my mother, Manda Matak, who instilled the courage and determination in me to pursue my career goals regardless of obstacles and challenges. I would like to acknowledge the staff of Security West, Brian Douglas, Richard Currie, and everyone who participated in the development of my first security company and individually brought great ideas to the table to save time and money in operations. There were too many late nights spent solving problems to ease the daily operations. We all learned and grew with the company.

INTRODUCTION: WHO AM I AND WHY SHOULD YOU LISTEN TO ME?

I got my first job in the security industry accidentally. I had just left my job working as a dispatcher for the North Vancouver RCMP and had finished my criminology undergraduate degree. I was undecided about where to go career-wise and the owner of a security company I had met offered me a job as general manager for his company.

I definitely had no idea what I was walking into nor did I have any knowledge about the private security industry. What I did bring to the table were superior organizational skills, a great personality, and no fear of the unknown. I used all these assets during my time with this security firm.

Thus, I began my tenure at a local security firm. But there was no future there; it was a small company owned by two men who shared partnership duties but were in complete discord about how to operate the company. It was a chaotic, disorganized, sometimes concerning work environment. The company was unionized and I spent a lot of time working with the union to clean up management decisions that conflicted with union regulations.

During this time frame the business agents at the union recommended me as a manager to a national company looking to set up an office in British Columbia. At that time they were the largest

Canadian-owned private security firm, handling major security contracts that my previous employer was unable to take on. It was the next level of private security work and I had the privilege of setting up security at the Quintette Coal site at Tumbler Ridge, the Point Roberts terminal, and various other contract sites. As manager I built their business from zero employees to around 200 within a year and a half. This national company entered the BC marketplace.

During these two experiences I noticed one common problem that was costly to both organizations: A lack of training for the security staff in a formalized, standardized way. One company had a philosophy that training was critical to success so we were able to work with in-house training programs that covered main points, but training was not considered important within the industry in general nor by the licensing body.

Once I had accomplished my goal of putting that company on the map I decided to form my own business, Security West Ltd. As such I became the first female private security company owner in British Columbia. I was fortunate enough that I had built such a rapport with many clients that when I left they chose to turn over their expiring contracts to my new company. So we started with a good base, and good supervisory staff.

Nevertheless the industry was competitive, and we faced a lot of union negotiations and one major client bankruptcy. At that time my common-law partner and I sat in my office at night, realizing we had just lost all our funds due to that client's inability to pay, and we had to make a decision. I remember clearly sitting in our office on Homer Street saying, "Well, either we walk away or we push on against all odds and maybe someday laugh about this."

We did push on but I cannot honestly say we ever laughed about it. In order to survive we had to immediately review our operations and our critical cash shortage and find a solution.

That solution was to unify our staff, with whom we were close anyway, and work hand in hand on a regular basis. We became a team and worked together to make a profit.

We also had to change our invoicing system to a pre-delivery system. In other words, clients would be billed in advance of services so that the invoice was paid before the month was over. Everyone said our large government contracts would not agree to this, but they were wrong. Everyone cooperated and our little company survived and continued to do so until we sold to a national firm.

I was soon asked to sit on the local board of the Canadian Society for Industrial Security and to take on the part-time role of security programs coordinator at the Justice Institute of British Columbia. This was a joint program between Canadian Security Intelligence Service (CSIS) and the Continuing Education Department. I was contracted to research, develop, and write the foundation of the security guard training program; this course was the foundation of what is now a mandatory security guard training program in British Columbia. It was a wonderful opportunity to be one of the first security trainers in the province. I was fortunate to be able to travel and train staff at most of the large mine and mill sites within the province.

In addition to this, I wrote the security supervisor's course, and courses for retail security, hotel security, and investigators. I was contracted to write the radio dispatch course, the alarm course, and a locksmith course for the Government of Canada Entry Program. I wrote and developed courses for the Ministry of the Attorney General. I wrote and taught courses and seminars during Expo 86 on residential security issues faced by new bed and breakfast owners.

My company ended up specializing in mall and hotel security, with a secondary priority being securing downtown buildings that required access control. We operated a cost-effective mobile patrol that was allocated to supervisors and thus we were able to maintain supervisory control of our sites at night.

As a security company owner, I have set up security for the smallest client to special events to large contracts requiring special considerations. This industry has taken me across the country and to every type of possible corporate and architectural structure. It has been challenging and exciting and rewarding.

When I said I wanted to run a security company, I was told it wouldn't work because I was a woman.

When I started my business, I was told by many it would never succeed.

When my largest client went bankrupt, I was told we needed to close.

When I went to meet with the association of companies that were the bargaining representatives for union negotiations, I overheard the men in the room saying that I had kept a certain contract because of my feminine wiles, not the incredible strategy we put in place to keep the job. (A sad statement on the thinking of those men.)

The purpose of this book is to provide you with the tools to make an entry into the security industry in a successful manner while avoiding unnecessary financial losses, but the moral of my story is that you should not listen to naysayers; listen to yourself, trust your inner voice, and trust the ability you have to succeed. There is no such thing as "I can't."

WHY START A BUSINESS IN THE SECURITY INDUSTRY?

Do you like challenge? Are you interested in working in a field that is constantly evolving requiring the same of you; an industry that will expose you to such a variation of business that few other industries do; an exciting, fast-paced environment? Security is all of these things and more. No day brings the same problems or resolutions.

Many people enter the security industry directly from a similar field, such as the military or policing. Many see this as a lateral-entry environment; one that requires little new training on their parts; one where they feel a relatively secure sense of belonging. Since it can seem restrictive in relation to licensing anyone from outside policing or the military, people from these backgrounds are more likely to enter it.

This overfamiliarity with the general idea of a career in security downplays perhaps the biggest and most important part of this service industry, which is customer relations. Policing and the military are enforcement environments with some recent emphasis on public relations and prevention, but business is all about customer relations and service needs. The security industry is a service industry — no different than janitorial services — just a different service that is being offered. It must always be remembered that the service is to the customer, the client. While law enforcement focuses

on the public perspective of the crime, security focuses on how the client wants to deal with these issues.

Successful companies work with the foundation of customer service as a priority. A proactive company needs assessment and service resolution is what you offer a client. This does not vary, from mobile patrols to major contracts. What is the problem? How is it being handled? How does the client want it to be handled? What recommendations can you make? What have you agreed on? Who of your staff can fit the requirements of this job to perform that mandate?

The security industry is one that provides manpower as a preventative presence. Enforcement can occur but only within the guidelines set by the client and these are often influenced by their mandate to draw the public to their location or their desired relationship with the public. Prevention is difficult if not impossible to measure, and therefore receives little acknowledgment. Rate increases often have to be justified and the competitive market has tended to keep the rates inflexible. Yet the industry is exciting and fulfilling and demanding.

1. Why the Security Business?

Security is often identified as the largest growth service industry in Canada, so there is plenty of room for new businesses.

Statistics Canada has provided this information:

"For many years, employment in the private security industry has exceeded that of public police officers. In 2006, this was the case for all provinces except Saskatchewan. There were about 102,000 private security personnel in Canada, compared to 68,000 police officers, representing about 3 private security personnel for every 2 police officers. Security guards made up 90% of private security personnel.

"While the rate of both police officers and private security personnel per 100,000 population increased between 2001 and 2006, private security grew much faster, up 15% compared to 3% for police officers. The increase in private security personnel was due to the growth in the number of security guards."[1]

"According to research firm IHS Inc., North and South America generated $46 billion in revenue last year. Asia was next with $33 billion, and the combined regions of Europe, the Middle East and Africa totaled $29 billion. Strong growth is predicted in all markets for the next few years."[2]

1 "Private Security and Public Policing," Statistics Canada, accessed November 2015. www.statcan.gc.ca/pub/85-002-x/2008010/article/10730-eng.htm
2 "Expect More Growth," Ralph C. Jensen, *Security Today*, accessed November 2015. https://security-today.com/Articles/2013/12/01/Expect-More-Growth.aspx

These numbers are reflective of the security industry across the product line and the service industry.

In times of recession, assets still have to be protected. Large industrial sites will combine technology along with manpower.

Guards' duties today reflect the increase of technology and security development — while many jobs are still straightforward "watch duty," many more require a set of specialized skills and training.

The industry has been in steady growth for the past 25 years. There are no lack of structures that need to be protected — from the individual residence to posh resort hotels to airports to strike situations.

2. Things to Think about When Starting a Security Business

Success and growth seems guaranteed in an industry that is growing at such a rapid rate and is double the size of public police. Nevertheless, few small companies survive the first five years of operation, in any industry.

Most often, people who start security businesses come from policing or military backgrounds. It is a natural fit for people retiring or leaving those careers early. However, previous policing or military experience does not mean they will be successful in security. Unlike policing, private enterprise succeeds in the hands of those who are proactive and creative with their business development.

The bottom line is that whether you provide security guards or janitors, you are in the service industry and not a paramilitary business. The job, with a security business, is to service the needs of clients through the rental of personnel, who in turn guard and secure a premises.

An understanding of security guards' legal rights and responsibilities is also a major consideration in operating a business of this nature; make sure that is part of training (discussed in Chapter 6).

3. Research and Learn about the Business

It is helpful to have some knowledge of the private security industry to learn how you can sell your services to a wider audience. Some people come directly from the industry where they were security guards or supervisors and start their own businesses. Others were managers in the industry or in a related position that required hiring contract guards.

This is a business that operates 24/7. You will be expected to provide a service to accommodate these hours.

The largest growth within the private security industry is with guard service alone or guard service in combination with security/access systems. Regardless of the sophistication of the security system, manpower is still required to respond to an alarm.

I was fortunate to learn my managerial skills within a small local company and then the largest Canadian company at the time who provided services to a much larger scope of clientele. If you are a security officer with no managerial experience, my recommendation is that you take some training in operating a small business along with courses to enhance your security knowledge. At present, the American Society for Industrial Security offers a program for managers that is recognized worldwide. Canada no longer offers a similar course. The more you learn about the various aspects of the industry and the services you can provide, the more you will be seen as a knowledgeable professional, and the greater will be your successes in this industry.

Some jobs are smaller and stable and others are large contracts that require constant staff adjustments, communications, and client relations and yet the pricing for both is often the same. Security is often seen as a necessary evil so it is not often valued highly, making charge-out rates hard to raise. Large bids often go to tender and to the lowest bidder. This is simply an unfortunate fact of life. Do your research on your competitors; know what rates are at the present time; do not confuse the charge-out rate as being your net profit; this is a highly competitive, rate-based industry. The industry has operated for too long with unskilled personnel, lack of proper training, and low-bid mentality. Do not fall into this trap. Decide what your margins need to be to operate a successful business and stick to them.

This is an industry that generally requires the services to be completed before invoicing occurs. This means generally a 30-day wait for payment after invoicing. Operating capital is required to meet your staffing and overhead costs until receivables are collected.

Security is an intense, fast-moving business to operate. Requirements are rarely the same so each job presents new challenges. This business will take you across all industries and professions and you will meet the most interesting people on that journey. No other business will give you access to such a diversity of clientele. One day you will be in a hard hat touring the construction of a new high-rise; the next day at a marina discussing methods of access control; the third day at a university reviewing its requirements. Demands will be intense when you start. Be ready, and have systems in place so it will be profitable to take on new challenges.

4. What Types of Services Security Companies Offer

What services does a security company offer? These can be any of the following:

1. **Security guards for contract positions:** Private security guards are contracted by various organizations to protect assets and/or personnel. These are generally known as stationary guards and are located at all kinds of establishments to provided access control, general patrolling of the site, key control, escort duty, and loss prevention in some cases. Often used for special events to provide a safe atmosphere and to prevent problems, and when required, to enforce the rules of the organization.

2. **Mobile patrols:** Mobile security patrols traditionally are used by clients that wanted a security presence at their location but only at random times. Often insurance requirements indicated that a form of security was present. Mobile patrols provide the guard and a vehicle and in some cases dogs to patrol the site for a preestablished period of time. Some patrols are simply a drive-by and others require the guard to exit the vehicle and do a walkthrough of the site. In Vancouver, BC, mobile patrols are often set up in residential communities to provide a continuous presence as a deterrent — in addition to regular policing. The patrols are paid by the community. Often mobile patrol officers are also used as supervisors to attend to emergencies for the company.

3. **Community patrols:** Mobile and stationary officers that are hired by specific communities to provide roving patrols within that community. Their duties generally involve deterrence of break-ins and prevention of personal assaults.

4. **Uniformed personnel:** Uniformed security are used in locations where visibility of the security guard is a primary concern for the client; this requirement is to encourage prevention and to visibly state that enforcement will occur.

5. **Plainclothes personnel:** Security officers are often put in business attire in buildings where their primary responsibility is access control and public relations or loss prevention.

6. **Access duty:** Security staff are often hired for special events or locations where strict enforcement of access to the site is

required. This may or may not be part of an entire technological access system.

7. **Hotel security:** Security officers are hired to perform duties within hotel environments that may include first aid, access control, fraud prevention, special events security, and so on.

   "Hotels must foster an inviting atmosphere for guests while ensuring safety and security. Presenting security personnel in a customer service role with officers dressed in upscale business clothing rather than traditional police- or military-style uniform, makes for a more accessible presence. This careful balance of customer service and security requires experience, specialized training and supervision. When your guests feel that they are both welcome and watched-over, they will feel more comfortable.

   "Ensuring that the right type of person occupies this customer-centric security role is also important. It is important to identify candidates through selective recruiting resources like hospitality and concierge associations and conduct extensive interviewing to ensure they possess a high aptitude for customer interaction."[3]

8. **Mall security:** Security within malls is to ensure the positive use of the mall shopping environment by all customers. Officers patrol the mall regularly, maintain information to assist customers, patrol exteriors, enforce parking issues on the site, work with police regularly in relation to shoplifting and theft matters and, more recently, threats of terrorism.

9. **Airport security:** Airport security today is a major concern for all countries and all travelers. Officers are required to screen travelers often with the aid of scanning equipment, check personal luggage and handbags, provide reasons to airport police as to suspect travelers, and handle all other matters that arise. This is a serious position that to this date is often sadly underpaid and does not result in stable security staff.

10. **Loss prevention officers:** Security guards that are trained to work in the retail industry specifically; often working in plainclothes to arrest shoplifters and coordinate the risk management and controls within respective departments.

11. **Construction security:** Construction security is most often at night; site protection is required after hours to ensure no break-ins or theft.

---

3 "Identifying 9 Solutions to Key Hotel Security Concerns," Bob Chartier, *Security Magazine*, accessed November 2015. www.securitymagazine.com/articles/85653-identifying-9-solutions-hotel-security-concerns

12. **Postsecondary campus, university, and college security:** Academic environments use security 24/7 and security officers maybe involved in escort duties, lock and key control maintenance, campus vehicle patrols, foot patrols, and enforcement

13. **Security consulting services:** Security companies are often providing consulting services to their clients. This is a separate area of endeavor that companies can move into as their access to clients is across the board and the opportunity to provide security plans for a fee is present.

14. **Bike patrols:** For large areas bike patrols are more common today as they can access areas faster than vehicles and can be present in areas where vehicles are not welcome.

15. **k9 services:** Security officers that work with trained dogs for private organizations. Often dogs are used on mobile patrols and drug searches.

16. **Concierge officers:** Often the concierge is expected to perform security duties by limiting access to the location to those with approval or the verification of guests attending the location.

17. **Emergency response:** Today many cities require the first response to an alarm be a security person. Once the building is checked, and if there has been a break-in, then the police arrive. This is an effective way of using police resources for critical incidents and allowing the false alarm problem to be billed accordingly.

18. **Special events security:** Concerts, VIP arrivals, and celebrities often require additional security. Each type of special event requires a certain type of training and personality be provided to the client.

In addition to these standard guard-related services, many companies expand into alarm, lock, and investigative services. While this book may include these services as additions to the security services offered, these are different types of businesses that often require trades training or professional training. This book is focusing on the security officer (guard) industry which is manpower-based.

In the following chapters, we are going to review client relations, costing templates, staffing, basic training requirements, marketing for your business, operations, and finally we are going to take a hard look at why security businesses fail so that you can hopefully avoid any pitfalls. Read this book in full before you start your company so that you lay a solid foundation for success.

STARTING YOUR BUSINESS: ORGANIZATIONAL ISSUES

2

Many small businesses start with a great idea and a passionate owner but discover organizational issues as the business challenges them. Often, as each crisis arises or each problem has to be tackled, the owner/manager discovers new rules he or she has to put into place, precedents that need to be maintained for future reference, or preventative strategies he or she has stumbled across. Let's start with the basics of how to start and operate a security business; let's get organized.

1. Licensing

The first place to start is to research your local federal, and state or provincial requirements in terms of licensing. Often to obtain a security business license you have to clear criminal records checks, financial checks, and in some locations an interview with the appropriate registrar or licensing regulator. Without being able to clear these criteria you will not be able to own and operate a security company. In the US, 50 states equates to 50 different policies; in Canada, each province and territory exhibits different requirements. It is your responsibility to research and understand your local requirements.

1.1 City licensing

Most cities require that a business carry a business license to operate in that jurisdiction. These costs can vary drastically from one city to another.

This is a consideration when deciding on the location of your company. In some cases, the difference between city license costs can be more than $300 annually.

Some inspectors will require that your business license be kept in a publicly visible location at your office address; others are not concerned as much with visibility. Some contract jobs require you to obtain a business license for the city in which the contract job is located if the city or town is different from that of your business office. You may end up with multiple city licenses due to the nature and location of respective job sites and requirements outlined on public tenders.

2. Insurance Requirements and Restrictions

In places such as British Columbia, proof of adequate insurance is mandatory with license renewal. But this change is relatively new. Some provinces require investigators to also carry Errors and Omissions Liability insurance along with fire/general liability insurance. Some insurers carry special restrictions if weapons are involved, or if dogs are used. You may live in a state, province, or territory where insurance is not required and this will save you anywhere between $1,100 to $5,000 annually.

It is critical to have insurance as this is a high-risk industry. It is also important to note that not all insurers will cover security companies — regardless of what form — alarm, investigative, locksmith, and so on. The earlier you research your accessibility and cost of insurance coverage, the better information you'll have with which to decide whether to open and operate this type of business.

3. Company Structure

An often overlooked consideration when commencing a security company is what the corporate structure is going to be. Are you a one-person operation and do you plan to limit your activities? Or are you a visionary who wants to build a strong security company with lots of employees? These considerations will affect whether you choose to be a sole proprietor or run a limited company. This is a decision that requires you to consult with legal advisors and accountants. They will assist you in determining the pros and cons of which route to take.

Is your company going to be a partnership? If so, have you clearly outlined each partner's duties? Do you share identical or complementary strengths? Many partnerships fail because each individual approaches the relationship with unreal expectations of the other partner. These situations end up messy and can be counterproductive. Sort this out to begin with, and put it in writing in a legal partnership agreement. Review the partners' duties and responsibilities on a regular basis. A partnership can double your growth and productivity but it can also be the demise of a business. Be clear, concise, and focused.

Whichever structure you choose to follow, develop a flow chart that outlines duties, strategic alliances, and planning for growth. This is something you can incorporate into your employee handbook at a later date.

TABLE 1
SECURITY COMPANY STRUCTURE

4. Staffing and Support Networks

Deciding to start a company requires you to build your support network prior to opening the door. Pick your strategic liaison partners:

An accountant that can provide costing advice as well as taxation planning; a lawyer that understands contract law, employee law, and can provide incorporation services, if required. These two alliances will become the two most important in the long run.

After this you need to decide who is going to do the administrative work. Most small-business people assign themselves this job in the beginning. This can inadvertently affect your business in a negative way. If you actually enjoy the security work but start to find yourself bogged down by the paperwork, one or the other will suffer from inattention. It is not always affordable at the beginning to hire full-time help but these days virtual assistants are available for reasonable costs.

5. Administration

The goal of the majority of people entering business is to develop their business into a lifestyle that includes financial freedom and greater flexibility of time. In general, this possibility is a myth. Running your own business involves a great commitment of your personal time, energy, and where a family is involved, their understanding and support. One way to ensure less troubleshooting and fewer crises is to streamline communication (even as you grow) between the various departments. We have provided you with standard forms that you can incorporate into your business and modify as required to ensure good records management, on the download kit that came with this book.

You will note that there is an index that identifies what each form is used for. By implementing these forms into your system you will save hours of time in keeping track of client relations, guard hours, invoicing, scheduling, and staff management.

Standardized forms remove the possibility of miscommunications which result when notes are written on pieces of paper or transmitted verbally. Have the forms on each computer and train the staff in which one to use; set up a forms drawer for different staff to grab one when needed; this is often faster than printing them from the computer. Keep the masters on a disc or in a master binder. Change the date on the forms every time you upgrade or alter them to ensure you are always using the most current versions.

5.1 Finances

Perhaps the single most important decision of your business life, other than the decision to break into the security industry, is to find a banker you can work with. The traditional approach is to go to your local bank and/or others and obtain a line of credit for your business. I always found that difficult to do, so I decided to be creative and develop a detailed business plan. I mailed it to the banks I researched and selected, and asked them to contact me if they were interested.

That is how I ended up with three interested bankers and chose the one I felt was most compatible to my situation. This will save you a lot of time and possible discouragement in the search for a bank.

The largest objection I used to come across was that it was a service industry and as such had no real assets. I spent a lot of time countering that argument with signed contracts and such. Finally I decided to switch over the roles, and would only talk to those banks that were interested.

Accountants are part of the strategic alliance group you want to form. If you are not a numbers person, then you must have an accountant on your side from the beginning. An accountant can help you set up your internal systems, refer a bookkeeper to you, complete all your year-ends, and keep you on track. An annual review will help you understand where your money is being spent and where you may want to look at some reductions or changes. Do not pick the accountant because he or she seems nice. Check out the preson's credentials and make sure he or she understands the industry you are going into and the margins involved in it.

In order to be paid you have to provide your clients with invoices. Today, most small companies use a form of a computerized accounting package that helps them keep account payables and receivables organized. This is much easier than doing ledgers by hand. I am not going to make recommendations here, but I will suggest that you have your program ready to go before you open your doors and start your first job.

My invoicing always included an accurate print out of the days, hours, and guards that worked the site and the invoice would then reflect the total number of hours multiplied by the charge-out rate; any statutory holidays or overtime were shown as separate categories as were special requests. The invoice should state clearly what is being charged and supported by a backup schedule printout so that there is no delay in payment.

With each invoice we always attached a client evaluation report so we could receive feedback from the clients on a regular basis (see Sample 1).

CLIENT EVALUATION REPORT

Client Evaluation Report

CLIENT _____   CONTRACT _____

MONTH _____   CONTRACT MGR _____

Dear Sir/Madam:

We would appreciate your assistance in the completion of this monthly report. It only takes a few moments and ensures continual excellence in the security service.

PLEASE CIRCLE THE NUMBER WHICH BEST REPRESENTS YOUR EVALUATION IN EACH OF THE AREAS NOTED BELOW:

(Note: A 10 is excellent and a 00 is very poor)

PUNCTUALITY:	10	09	08	07	06	05	04	03	02	01	00
PUBLIC RELATIONS:	10	09	08	07	06	05	04	03	02	01	00
KNOWLEDGE OF JOB:	10	09	08	07	06	05	04	03	02	01	00
SUPERVISION:	10	09	08	07	06	05	04	03	02	01	00
RESPONSE FROM MANAGEMENT	10	09	08	07	06	05	04	03	02	01	00

Please use the following area for any further comments you may have in regards to any of the above areas of anything that you would like to bring to our attention: _____

_____

_____

_____

Thank you in advance for your assistance in this evaluation.

CC: 1-Supervisor
    2-Operations Supervisor
    3-Operation Administration
    4-Red File (original)
    5-Blue Binder (when completed)

You will note that the Client Evaluation Report form is copied to all the parties involved in the implementation of security. If there are issues to be dealt with, then operations works to resolve it.

5.2 Payroll

I have had the good fortune to operate a union and nonunion security company. The requirements for both involved excellent record keeping and verification of hours. This would involve time sheets being sent in weekly (your payroll may be biweekly or monthly but this system works for both) on a Monday morning, checked against the sites' information (often there were book-offs, changes) and then signed off by operations for payroll to handle.

The margins in the industry are tight, so ensuring accuracy of payment and charge-out rates is primary.

Keeping track of changes can become burdensome the larger your company gets. See Samples 2 through 9 for samples of forms you can use to keep track of the details. These forms, along with many more, are also on the download kit included with this book for your use.

5.3 Pricing

How do you determine pricing? Call your competition and ask for quotes on various special events and such. You get to play a private detective here; fake your identity and get some information, from the smallest competitor to the largest. Decide where your pricing should fit in based on what competitors charge, how your company and offerings differ, and what you can afford.

Ensuring that you cost out your staff properly is critical to long-term success. Oftentimes, explaining to your clients the cost of operations can assist you in increasing rates or, in the case of tenders, where they require breakdowns you will be prepared. Guard cost charts also assist the management in understanding their operational staffing costs and profit margins. See Sample 10 for a guard costing worksheet.

Our chart includes union costs which at one time were charged at .35 per hour, but you may have a different cost to insert here. These worksheets help you focus on the cost of the guard at each site and what your rate should be; it also helps you adjust your rates due to various increases in costs. It is a simple method to determine your profit margins on each job based on hours.

If you choose to branch into other services, you can use the same template to determine cost and profit margins.

PAYROLL DATA

Payroll Data

	1	2	3	4	5	6	7	8	9	10	11	12	13	14	15	16	17	18	19	20	21	22	23	24	25	26	27	28	29	30	31	Total Hours
ST.																																
OT.																																
SH.																																
TT.																																
ST.																																
OT.																																
SH.																																
TT.																																
ST.																																
OT.																																
SH.																																
TT.																																

NAME: _____

PAY PERIOD FROM: _____ TO: _____

EMPLOYEE # _____

DATE: _____

EARNINGS:	RATE:	HOURS:	AMOUNT:
Regular Time			
Overtime			
Doubletime			
Stat Holiday worked			
Travel Time			
Short Change			
Short Shift			
Mobile Premium			
Guard Dog			
Travel Allowance			
Private Car Allowance			
Stat Holiday (___%)			
Vacation/Holiday (___%)			
Miscellaneous			

Nontaxable Monies:
Meal Allowance
Reimbursements
Miscellaneous

DEDUCTIONS:	AMOUNT:
CPP/pension	
UIC	
Income Tax	
Licenses	
Medical	
Miscellaneous	

TOTAL DEDUCTIONS: _____

NET PAY: _____

GROSS PAY: _____

SAMPLE 3
PAYROLL DEDUCTION

Payroll Deduction

NAME: _____   DATE: _____

I hereby authorize _____, to deduct from my paycheck issued on
[Company Name]
_____the sum of $_____.

This deduction is for _____
_____
_____

I further agree and understand that any balance outstanding will be deducted from my final paycheck on termination of employment.

_____   _____
Employee   Company Name

_____
Date

CC: Payroll
     Employee's Time Sheet file

PAYROLL DEDUCTION: VEHICLE

[Insert Company Letterhead]

Payroll Deduction

I, _____, hereby authorize _____ to deduct from
                                                      [Company Name]
my paycheck all and any costs resulting from negligence on my part which results
in damage being done to any vehicle I am operating (which is owned or leased by
_____ whilst in the employ of _____.
     [Company Name]   [Company Name]

DATE: _____   SIGNATURE: _____

                                WITNESSED BY: _____

TIME SHEET

Time Sheet

Employee Name: _____

Pay Period From: _____

Employee Number: _____

To: _____

Day	Date (MM/DD/YY)	Location	Shift	Regular Time	Dog Handling	Car Patrol	Overtime*	Stat Holiday	Transport Allowance	Meal Allowance	Dry Cleaning
Sunday											
Monday											
Tuesday											
Wednesday											
Thursday											
Friday											
Saturday											

* You will not be paid for overtime unless you explain what it is for: _____

Rate of Pay Increase

DATE: _____

Name: _____

Employee #: _____

Old Rate: _____

New Rate: _____   Effective: _____

Reason: _____
_____
_____
_____

_____   _____
Personnel   Manager

SAMPLE 7
PETTY CASH VOUCHER

No. _____ $ _____

PETTY CASH VOUCHER

Date _____

For _____

_____

_____

Charge to _____

ACCOUNT

_____

APPROVED BY _____   RECEIVED BY _____
(Petty Cashier)

- -

No. _____ $ _____

PETTY CASH VOUCHER

Date _____

For _____

_____

_____

Charge to _____

ACCOUNT

_____

APPROVED BY _____   RECEIVED BY _____
(Petty Cashier)

SUMMARY OF AUTO EXPENSES

Summary of Auto Expenses

For the month of _____

Employee: _____

Location: _____

Branch: _____

Balance brought forward from last month $_____

Add mileage claim   _____

Less: Expenses to be paid by _____ (attach all receipts)

Car Payment   _____

Gas   _____

Insurance   _____

Auto Repair   _____

Parking   _____

                                    TOTAL $_____

Balance carried forward to next month: $_____

_____
Signature

SAMPLE 9
SHORTAGE OF WORK HOURS

To: _____

Re: Hours of Work

We regret that owing to lack of work, we are unable to guarantee to you 40 hours per week. Under the circumstances, you may exercise your choice of either going on part-time or being terminated for lack of work. Should you choose part-time work for this reason, you will be given preference over all part-time employees for full-time work when it becomes available.

Detach

To: [Company Name]

In view of the circumstances outlined above, I wish to advise you of my intention as follows:

[   ]   Elect part-time status

[   ]   Elect termination owing to lack of work and request
        Record of Employment form

_____
Signature

If you elected termination for lack of work, please return your security employee's license to _____ for filing until required and return uniform items.
                          [Company Name]

GUARD COSTS

	Regular	Overtime	Statutory Holiday
Hourly Rate: ___% Annual Holiday Pay ___% Statutory Holiday Pay			
Subtotal			
Union Assessment Government Assessment			
Subtotal			
Overhead			
Profit			
Total Charge-out Rate			

5.4 Business set-up

Decisions around business set-up will reflect the amount of capital you are willing to put out until your costs are covered. My advice to all small businesses is to keep it simple, keep it fluid, and focus on the service. Very few clients will be coming to your office and there really is no need to impress anymore. As one client of mine said many years ago, "I don't care if you work out of your house as long as you can provide the service I need."

Yes, you can work out of your home. But if you plan to do this, I suggest you have a completely separate environment for your business; a separate door for people to come and go from; and a distinct division between personal and professional. However, I do not actually recommend running a security business from your house. The turnover of staff is enormous which will ultimately mean that hundreds of people that you know little or barely anything about will be coming to your residence and inevitably interacting with your family.

While we worked and spent a lot of energy getting to know our staff, ultimately we became too large to be that personal. At that point only our K9 staff had access to our personal home address because they had to pick up the dogs and drop them off there. I am a firm believer in your home being your sanctuary and a safe place to retreat to when you feel the world is beating you up. So, look for an office close to home that is reasonably priced. Do not go for flash, and you do not have to be in the middle of the downtown core. You need to be accessible to your staff. You will be going to visit your clients; rarely will they come to you.

Everyone today is operating with cell phones and that is great, but again have one for work only. You need to set boundaries on how and when you are contacted as this is a 24/7 business.

Overhead costs need to be kept to a minimum. When you start the business and you have decided what security service you will start with, focus on meeting those needs. An office and a phone are your basics.

A computer and an Internet connection are also mandatory today. Computers can save you hours of time and pretty well run your entire business. Keep your personal and business information on separate computers. Make sure you have a backup for your office system. Speaking from experience, you will lose your data at the worst possible moment if you don't back up your data regularly.

6. Business Plan

Before you go into any business, you should think through all of the possibilities. How will you make money, what kind of staff will you employ, where will your office be, and what kind of marketing will you do?

When all is said and done, a security company serves three masters: the clients, the owner, and the employees. Keep this in mind as you begin to write a plan for your business. And do write it out as you go through and when you're done this book. You will need to have thought through all the questions if you want to get money from a bank; it will also help you to have things planned for in advance.

See Sample 11 for an example of a business plan you can refer to as you write your own.

BUSINESS PLAN TEMPLATE

THE ABC AGENCY

MARCH 20XX

THIS DOCUMENT CONTAINS CONFIDENTIAL AND PROPRIETARY INFORMATION BELONGING EXCLUSIVELY TO THE ABC AGENCY.

This is a business plan. It does not imply an offering of securities.

TABLE OF CONTENTS

I.   INTRODUCTION

Executive Summary

The ABC Agency will provide investigation and surveillance services to the retail community, business industry, and the general public. Through utilization of the image and formidable reputations in all advertising materials a corporate image will be developed. Tradition, integrity, creativity, and attention to detail, combined with the flair of the owner's approach to investigations will provide an imposing competitor.

- Today's insecure times pose a threat to personal safety and financial security, creating a demand for private investigators, risk managers, and security professionals.
- In the past year alone, various companies contracted $7.3 million worth of security services.
- Approximately 80 percent of the retail community will use some form of security services.
- The general public has become concerned about personal safety.
- More and more families are seeking security systems.
- Terrorism has increased public awareness for security.
- Policing costs are inhibiting the growth of public police focusing on the private arena for greater assistance, training, and credibility.

The business is presently operated as home-based with the strategic location: Burnaby. The corporate structure allows accessibility to property and local market availability. Additionally, it will benefit from security guard clientele associated with one of its corporate partners.

I, Bob Smith, will fulfill the positions of owner and key person. I have 20 years experience in policing, training, program development, and business management. I have instructed in the field of law, report writing, surveillance, and sales at various local schools and colleges. I have served on various industry and community boards which have expanded the field of opportunities. I am currently active on various community boards and have built a positive community reputation based on my volunteer involvements.

The business has been financed by myself and will look towards a small line of credit within the next few months. I expect to see a 20 percent profit after the first year of operation, and a 35 percent profit after the second year. This varies with the amount of contract labor engaged.

II.   BUSINESS CONCEPTS

Description of Business Venture

The name of the business is The ABC Agency. A full range of security products and services from personal to corporate will be offered. These services are discussed in detail in the Marketing Plan.

The corporate structure of The ABC Agency will be as a division of a corporate entity — ABC Inc. owned solely by myself. The office will be located at 123 Main Street, Burnaby, BC. The location provides local address image and telephone numbers that will appeal to customers seeking local business contracts.

I will be opening a line of credit for the business which will be secured by a term deposit. Planned sales for the first year of the business are $100,000.

Key personnel at this time will be myself and two other key people to encompass administrative and operational areas. Disability and liability insurance has been arranged and key person insurance are in place.

Licenses and bonding in accordance with the Attorney General's regulations are required both for the business and personally. These have been obtained. A fully equipped office has been set up. A formal mailing address is established at PO Box 123, Burnaby, BC V5V 5V5. The corporate image has been established through letterhead and our website www.TheABC Agency.com. A potential client listing has been obtained and rates established. Advertising has been arranged in several retail and professional publications as outlined in the Marketing Plan.

The ABC Agency will excel because of my extensive knowledge and experience in the field of investigations. In addition, I am educated and experienced in business management. Competitive pricing, availability, thoroughness, accuracy, report preparation, knowledge, professionalism, and timeliness are critical variables to success in this business. Detailed and consistent membership, sales, and promotions will contribute to success. Hard work, commitment, and "pit-bull" determination will inspire the business. A balanced approach to business, family life, and health will be the foundation of the business.

Description of Industry

This business is part of the private-policing, security-service industry that services both small and large business as well as individuals. These services are required by corporations, retail organizations, hotels, and the general public. Business operations run from very small (one person) to large organizations. The advantages of a small operation is that it can be subcontracted to a larger security company.

The trend of this industry is high growth. Personal protection issues and hotel security.

The biggest obstacle to overcome in obtaining business is the stigma that retired police officers are the best qualified and therefore, the best security people.

Special features of this business will be: The "pit-bull approach" to problem-solving, a small but thorough business, computerization, and 24-hour access. The ABC Agency also fits perfectly into a niche that very few companies address — business detail security personnel.

The private policing industry features 20 percent annual growth in Canada — a figure cited in *Security Magazine*. This publication regularly reviews the growth of various segments of the private-policing industry.

Vision and Mission Statements

The vision of this business is to provide first-rate security, consulting, and risk-management services. A secondary phase will commence manpower operations services. The immediate target market will be the retail sector in order to provide a foundation for operations. During the next six months, The ABC Agency will focus on building the retail investigative market prior to the Christmas season. During the first year, a lot of energy will be spent on networking, joining community organizations,

4

building support staff, marketing, and direct sales. By the end of year one, The ABC Agency plans to be in the office on a full-time basis.

Plans for the long-term development of the business: This part of the business would offer more extensive tech services.

It is also a goal of The ABC Agency to form a training academy, complete with a security guard training manual that can be marketed within and outside of the training academy.

My personal goal is to build this business within the business community and to build a financial base on which to offer pro-bono services — specializing in consumer advocacy.

Mission Statement

"To provide a full range of high-quality security and risk-management services with knowledge, integrity, and professionalism."

The ABC Agency will promote this image of integrity and knowledge through the use of a logo. The business will maintain professionalism in all its dealings and will operate with a Code of Ethics as outlined below.

Code of Ethics:

The ABC Agency will:

- Provide thorough and accurate solutions to client demands.
- Operate at all times with integrity.
- Offer competitive pricing.
- Provide information in a timely manner.
- Disengage from security jobs that conflict with Mission Statement.
- Expect clients at all times to be honest with their information.
- Support community endeavors with an eye to community leadership.
- Not engage in any illegal behavior to obtain information.

Business Goals

- The ABC Agency will break even in the third quarter of operations.
- After the first year, the operating line of credit will be for emergency use only.
- Profits will be left in the operating account to operate with.
- The first year of operations will enable myself to earn $36,000, purchase a new vehicle, and maintain the line of credit at a $0 balance.
- By the second year of business I would earn $46,000 per annum and work an average of 60 hours per week.
- The second year will focus on increasing the security work that can be contracted out to provide greater revenues.
- By the third year of business my earnings would increase by 25 percent and the business would become renowned as a security leader within the business community and the general public.

The first year of business sales are expected to be $100,000 increasing to $500,000 within five years. My goal is that The ABC Agency generates a personal income of $150,000/year after five years.

The business will be in the top ten companies in the British Columbia market due to experience, knowledge, and public relations. The ABC Agency will become one of the leaders in the industry in terms of legislative changes, training, and program development.

Strategic Alliances

The business has developed the following strategic alliances to assist in the development of its goals.

1. An alliance with XYZ Alarm Systems for all CCTV or undercover surveillance equipment to be installed.

2. An alliance with Jane Doe, web designer, for all computer-related activities.

3. An alliance with Joe Smith, a litigation lawyer, to provide legal civil advice.

4. An alliance with Ray Doe, a chartered accountant, to oversee the business finances.

5. An alliance with various security firms to promote and share all work with each other in our respective regions.

6. Marketing alliances with various local coffee houses to display and maintain company brochures for the general public.

III. MARKETING PLAN

Service Description

Security services vary according to the industry that seeks this form of assistance. The ABC Agency will provide services to the business community, the corporate environment, and private individuals.

Application of Service

The ABC Agency will provide services according to the customer needs from the detailed list below.

Services for the BUSINESS COMMUNITY:

FRAUD: Investigations common to missing persons, theft, real estate, and bankruptcies.

Services for the CORPORATE and RETAIL SECTORS:

UNDERCOVER PERSONNEL: Staff working independently, or as a team capable of assuming various identities within organizations.

Industry and Market Analysis

Industry Description

The ABC Agency will be operating in the business and private-policing (security) industry. Ministry of Attorney General requirements are that security firms be regulated under the Security Programs Division and therefore, they become part and parcel of the security industry.

Market Segmentation

The industry segments can be broken down as follows:

- Business
- Retail
- Community
- Personal

Growth and Trends

The slow development of public law enforcement agencies in the United States, combined with the steady escalation of crime problems in an increasingly urban and industrialized society, created "security" needs which were met by what might be called the first professional private-policing responses in the second half of the 19th Century. In the 1850s Allan Pinkerton, a copper from Scotland and the Chicago police department's first detective, established one of the oldest and still largest private security operations in the United States. Today it has more than 40,000 employees. Since that day, the growth of private policing has risen steadily. In Canada, recent statistics show an average 20 percent growth over the past ten years.

Society has in recent times relied almost exclusively on the police and other arms of the criminal justice system to prevent and control crime, but today the sheer volume of crime and its cost, along with budget cutbacks in the public sector, have overtrained public law enforcement agencies. Investigators, therefore, play a greater role in prevention and control of crime than ever before.

Expenditures in private policing today exceed $30 billion annually. The market is competitive but given the growth of public and corporate crime, and the legislative changes that will be more restrictive in terms of licensing — the market is far from saturated.

Barriers

For new businesses there are barriers that have to be overcome. One is the requirement for licensing stipulated by law. The other change that is anticipated in the year 20XX is that all persons wishing to become security guards will be required to complete a basic course before they will be permitted to apply for licensing. This has been approved by the Security Company Association in conjunction with representatives from the local colleges.

I have already met all the requirements for licensing and have obtained all the applicable licenses.

Competition

Competitive Environment

Research indicates that there are 63 security companies operating in the Lower Mainland. All 63 were contacted. Of these, 45 percent responded to the survey, 14 percent would not participate, and 40 percent did not respond. These are comprised of everything from small to national companies. Services range from specialized to general and pricing ranges from $40 to $120 per hour. By far the largest portion of investigators are male, with backgrounds in police and military.

Of the 28 respondents one was immediately eliminated as the only service they provided was armored car. Of the remaining 27, four were in business less than five years, nine were in business six to ten years, and nine were in business longer than ten years. The remaining companies would not answer this question. The average rate cited was $15 per hour. Sixteen service options were listed and of the respondents 12 indicated they provided all of them. The rest indicated various groupings of the 16 service options. Forty-five percent of the companies stated that the reason their company was the best was the staff was ex-police, 30 percent stated they were "ex-police," and the remainder did not respond.

Major Competitors

The ABC Agency has identified the following firms as major competitors: Investigations Ltd., Investigative Services, and Protection Services. All these firms are owned and operated by one person. Their reputation has been built by the owner. Aside from Protection Services, which has 18 years of business operations, the other firms have been in business more than five years. All provide services within British Columbia. None of these firms lists a specialty service or competitive advantage.

Future Competition

Upcoming legislative changes will restrict entry into the industry until a training course has been completed. This at present is not required. A simple registration fee and application approval is all that is now required to operate a license. Two years policing or equivalent (not specified) background will enable a person to obtain a private investigator's license. Although the course will provide some obstacle, the growth of the industry will be a motivation for persons to enter. The market can manage competitive growth.

Strengths and Weaknesses of Competition

Major competitors have strength in the areas of years of business, corporate images, effective advertising and promotion. The weakness of the majority is that they operate exclusively for one company and when that work is reduced they suffer. Very few of these companies develop business outside that realm. The confidentiality of the business makes it almost impossible to determine whether the competition has performed poorly. Clients are hesitant to discuss investigative results except in extremely general terms. Another weakness is that the businesses operate in the ex-policing world — isolationist and exclusive. Often they overlook business opportunities outside of the "old boys network."

Competitive Strategy

The ABC Agency will be a fierce competitor due to its intense and extensive advertising program, community work, and positive public relations. Our business strengths will include one physical location to operate from, extensive existing networking for word-of-mouth referrals, an intense flyer distribution program, and aggressive sales planning. Our pricing is comparable and competitive. My background is impressive and will support clientele development. Additionally I am actively involved in the policing community — both ex and present. Past client references will speak of my professional and thorough approach to problem-solving and risk analysis.

Definition of Target Market

Demographic Description

In the first year of business The ABC Agency will target 16 major malls, 18 hotels, and 20 property firms.

Geographic Boundaries

Our services will be provided within the province of British Columbia in order to be competitive; although many times the actual investigations cross boundaries.

Anticipated Size of Target Market

The size of our start-up market is 16 malls, 18 hotels, and 20 property firms.

Anticipated Sales/Share of Target Market

It is estimated that The ABC Agency will capture 10 percent of the business market, 5 percent of the mall market, and 3 percent of the hotel market by the end of the first year.

Marketing Strategy

Company's Message Statement

The ABC Agency stands for a company that holds traditional values and techniques in high regard yet is creative, cunning, discreet, young, sharp, and intelligent.

Advertising & Promotion

The ABC Agency's strategy is multifold. We will concentrate as follows:

- Large ad in the Retail Directory issued November 20XX
- Ad in the Professional Services Directory issued October XX
- Regular monthly advertising in Retail Magazine
- Super page advertising is in place
- Flyer mail out to our target market the first week of April
- Flyer program for the rest of the year has been developed
- New business promo in the Business section of the newspaper
- Chamber of Commerce — new business promo

These are annual publications that are provided to the business community — in some cases free of charge. The financial plan reflects these costs under the month they become due.

Current memberships in several professional organizations will maintain a constant network.

Once the above is in place, focus will shift to include a radio interview and one other talk-show within the next three months. There is no cost to The ABC Agency.

The next consideration will be to do a business presentation for the local Chamber of Commerce. The company will also have the opportunity to chair and partially sponsor a local event during the Christmas season. This will give the company greater visibility in the community.

The ABC Agency will actively participate in super page advertising in the year 20XX for the Vancouver, Surrey, and Kelowna areas.

Strategic Alliances

The ABC Agency has strategic alliances in the retail and computer security fields.

Sales Strategy

Sales Forecast

The ABC Agency is forecasting $100,000 in sales the first year with the break-even point being $65,000 in sales arrived at by the third quarter.

Sales Organization

The ABC Agency's sales will be conducted primarily by myself. Two commissioned sales representatives familiar with the retail industry will be recruited to develop the retail investigations section. Target time will be for the Christmas season. An agreement will be prepared wherein they will receive a commission based on duration, value, and feasibility of the contract.

Sales Methods

Thirty sales calls a day for four days a week will be made and documented. From these 120 calls it is anticipated that eight to ten appointments will be made. A sales sheet has been developed that will be followed and then forwarded to administration for the updating of the mailing lists. This sheet will also be able to trace the originator of the call to determine commission allocation.

Each week, after the flyers have been distributed, calls will be made to that target industry. Although 10 percent of client calls are self-generated the majority will be the result of mailouts, cold-calling, and personal appointments

Customer Buying Pattern

Generally, it will take up to three months to close a large client. Clients generate repeat business when satisfied with the work.

Distribution Channel

In order to facilitate sales, one location has been selected to provide services and image to the clientele — Greater Vancouver from the Burnaby location. Physically it does not matter where the security guard is — the perception of location, however, is very important.

Order Fulfilment

The work must be carried out promptly and reports provided no later than one day after completion of an incident. This allows time for all disbursements to be tabulated and billing will be concurrent.

Customer Service Policy

The ABC Agency plans to be innovative in its approach to customer service by providing an evaluation report with the completed service. This provides the clients with the opportunity to express their feelings about how the work was conducted and gives the

10

company time to respond to specific issues. In the case of an incident, the clients may receive information that they feel does not fit their personal agenda. Clients will be reminded of the Agency's Code of Ethics and confirm that we investigate the facts not the fiction.

Market Research Summary

Primary Research:

- Complete market survey questionnaire/competition survey questionnaire.
- Contacted 100 top property firms.
- Examined how many PI firms there are in British Columbia and what services they provide.
- Spoke to various organization heads to determine needs within the Lower Mainland.
- Attended Security Association's meeting and spoke to the Chairperson.
- Spoke to past clients and prepared current list of prospects.
- Survey of competition.
- Located all publications that were available to potential buyers.
- Interviewed suppliers.
- Spoke to mentors and advisors.

Secondary Research:

- Reviewed trade magazines.
- Searched the Internet.
- Reviewed newspaper clippings.
- Attended at library and reviewed books on industry.
- Obtained materials from the criminology department at the university.
- Contacted Trade Board.
- Attended Business Center for written information.

Market Research Still to be Done

Research to be completed during the first year of operation:

- Contact businesses based on geographic areas to determine their needs.
- Speak to corporations regarding employee theft.
- Contact government agencies to determine contracting security services.

Marketing Critical Path

First Quarter:

- Mail brochures to malls in Burnaby, New Westminister, and Coquitlam.
- Mail brochures to property firms in Burnaby, New Westminister, and Coquitlam that are on the 100 list.
- Program 100 numbers in fax for faxing advertising.
- Join Trade Board.
- Put in place all annual advertising.
- Cold calling commences.
- Tidy mailing lists — verify addresses.
- Check government listings on the Internet.
- Develop year-to-date marketing plan.

<u>Second Quarter:</u>

- Refer to marketing plan agenda.
- Continue advertising.
- Yellow Page advertising.
- Cold calls.
- Work with local newspaper to develop a "consumer advocacy" column.
- Commence a free information newsletter for potential customers that will be sent out with the brochures initially.
- Tidy mailing lists for each category — verify addresses.
- Radio interview.

<u>Third Quarter:</u>

- Refer to marketing plan agenda.
- Follow-up on cold calling and flyer program.
- Reevaluate success of various marketing endeavors.

<u>Fourth Quarter:</u>

- Refer to marketing plan agenda.
- Develop mailing lists for newsletter only.
- Renew annual advertisement programs.
- Plan for client party — in business one year at office by invitation only.

IV.   OPERATIONS PLAN

Operations

Legal form of business

The legal form of the business will be an incorporated business, ABC Inc., owned solely by myself.

Regulations

The ABC Agency is required to obtain an annual license from the Ministry of the Attorney General for the corporate entity and its individual employees. A city business license is also required. The business will have tax and workers' compensation regulations. All licensing required for start-up have been obtained.

Business Records & Financial Controls

All business records files have been set up. Arrangements are being made to open a current account and a line of credit. No commitments have been made to date. Monthly books will be kept by myself. I have 15 years of experience operating Simply Accounting software.

Business Financing

All financing to date of the business has been by my personal funds.

Production

Production Methods

Business will commence immediately with myself performing the managerial tasks. Two operatives are presently being interviewed for licensing purposes should additional help be warranted by the end of the first quarter.

Costs

Services are available now and the business has been operating on a small scale.

Quality Control

Quality will be maintained through a hands-on approach during the first year of business, and thereafter by a process of regular evaluation of contractors and staff. Quality control of client satisfaction will be through in-person consultations and file-evaluation reports.

Equipment

Appendix D is a detailed list of capital equipment invested for the purpose of conducting business. [**Note:** *Appendix D is not included in this sample Business Plan.*]

Suppliers

Arrangements have been made with the following suppliers:

Company Courier	Online Services	Local newspaper
Mobility Company	Credit Bureau	Wholesale Company
Office Supplies	Medical Services Company	

Personnel and Management

Key People

During the first year, the business will operate with the following personnel:

Manager

> Responsible for overseeing all aspects of the business, including providing services and supervision of staff.

Office Manager — to be hired

> Responsible for running entire office. Mature seasoned professional wanted.

Security operations

All staff will be engaged on a casual basis and will be paid on contract rates that are billable to the specific job.

There will be no increase in administration staff for the next year. Investigative staff will be added dependant on the volume of surveillance work. Two "under supervision" investigators will be hired prior to the legislative changes scheduled for sometime in 20XX.

Outside Advisors, Consultants, Mentors

*[**Note:** List all your mentors here.]*

Lawyer - Mr. R. Lawyer, corporate adviser
Accountant - Mr. B. Accountant, Chartered Accountant

Risk Assessment

Competitors Reaction

The industry growth allows for new competitors with minimal impact. Continuity of the business is guaranteed due to strong networking personally and professionally. In other words, satisfied clients equals repeat business and referrals.

External Factors

Licensing changes anticipated for the year 20XX will make the selection of security staff more restrictive and may increase the waiting time to hire an employee. However, standardized training provides for better hiring prospects.

Internal Factors

Critical internal factors that may affect the business include a significant increase in sales or not meeting sales targets. In either case impact is minimal as workers are contracted for services rendered. Overhead is very low as the operations will be run from existing home office. If sales are not being met, then the agency would seek contract work from larger organizations.

Personal Time Budget

As the key person, I will expend a great deal of energy in the first quarter on marketing, direct sales, and building on an existing network. As a regular flow of work comes in, the emphasis will be spread more evenly between these activities and services provided.

Operations Critical Path

First Quarter:

- Select business name
- Meet with advisors
- Prepare letterhead
- Arrange support staff
- Set up suppliers
- Develop records management system
- Review information for van purchase
- Interview two security personnel

Second Quarter:

- Interview subcontractors
- Review goals and objectives
- Work with salespersons to meet weekly and review objectives
- Evaluate marketing plan
- Set up vehicle maintenance program

Third Quarter:

- Employee/contractor evaluations
- In-house training program
- Motivation seminar for all staff
- Examine profit-sharing options for employees

Fourth Quarter:

- Review business plan
- Examine need for investors
- Plan client party — one year celebration
- Prepare books for year end

V. FINANCIAL PLAN

Projected Cash Flow and Explanatory Notes

The financial analyses immediately follow this page, namely: Sensitivity Analysis: Realistic, Slow Start, Fast Start

CASH FLOW (REALISTIC)

a) The breakdown of dues is as follows:

September	Costco— $42.80
	Association — $125
	Canadian Society for Security — $200.63
November	American Society for Security — $170
May	Chamber of Commerce — $278

b) Insurance cost details are:

Disability	$89
Life	$99
Extended Health	$69
General	$68
Total	$325

c) Licenses are annual:

February	Ministry of Attorney General	$40 (Personal license)
December	City	$278 (Business license)
March	Ministry of Attorney General	$275 (Company license renewal)
May	Bond	$150 (Bond renewal)

d) Automotive payment:

The amounts reflected from November onward are based on the purchase of a 20XX vehicle.

e) Bad debts:

Bad debts are not reflected in the financial forecasting as our business requires retainers for all new customers. Corporate clients in the first year will be limited.

CASH FLOW (SLOW START)

All of the previously stated information will still apply with the following exceptions: Automotive purchase and subsequent payments would be delayed until February 20XX.

CASH FLOW (FAST START)

The only relevant changes here would be the inclusion of full-time office support starting in May, as well as a portion of the security work being contracted out. Therefore, this cash flow will show $21,500 paid to contract staff and $16,500 for the office support staff.

*[**Note:** You should add a Projected Income Statement and a Projected Balance Sheet here.]*

Break-even Analysis

Step 1:

Total Sales	$100,000
Cost of Sales	0
Gross Margin	$100,000

Step 2:

Gross Margin percentage $\dfrac{100,000}{100,000} = 100\%$

Gross Margin percentage = 1.00

Step 3:

Total Expenses $51,260

Step 4:

BEP Sales Level = $\dfrac{51,260}{1} = BEP = 51,260$

Summary:

The BEP Sales Level is $51,260. Our forecast for the year indicates sales in Year 1 of $100,000. Income Statement forecast indicates that break even will be achieved mid-way through the third quarter.

Financial Critical Path

First Quarter:

- Establish line of credit.
- Apply for Vendor Status.
- Set up computer account.
- Meet with accountant and lawyer.
- Renew Credit Bureau membership.
- Obtain and organize necessary office supplies.
- Prepare proposal for investors to increase business opportunities.

Second Quarter:

- Do interim financial statements.
- Review statements with accountant.
- Cash injection for Christmas promotion.
- Review cash-flow forecasts for tracking.

Third Quarter:

- Develop Board of Advisors.

Fourth Quarter:

- Meet with banker to review status of accounts.
- Prepare year-end financial statements.
- Review and assess accuracy of Year 2 projections.

Personal Financial Information

I have owned my residence for the past 25 years.

Personal Life Insurance:	Term	$400,000
	Whole	$150,000
Disability Insurance:	$3,000/month	
Household Insurance:	Yes	
Professional Liability Insurance:	Yes	
Current Will:	Yes	
Trusts, Guardians, Other:	No	
Lawyer:	R. Lawyer	
Accountant:	B. Accountant	

*[**Note:** You should add a Personal Projected Cash Flow and Personal Net Worth here.]*

EXPENSES TO DATE:

ALL ITEMS PAID FOR

1.	MINISTRY OF ATTORNEY GENERAL LICENSING	$500.00
2.	BOND	150.00
3.	ONLINE (COMPUTER PROGRAM)	100.00
4.	THE CORPORATES	163.25
5.	TELEPHONE	45.99
6.	FAX LINE	40.80
7.	SECURITY ANNUAL PUBLICATION	53.50
8.	SECURITY MAGAZINE	107.86
9.	PERSONAL LICENSE	60.00
10.	COMPUTER UPGRADE	172.11
	TOTAL;	$1,393.51

ITEMS ORDERED BUT NOT YET PAID:

1. SECURITY ADVERTISING $440.00 (MIN AD)

2. EQUIFAX $96.00 AND MEMBERSHIP FEE $17.10 PER MONTH

3. LETTERHEAD, BUSINESS CARDS — $500.00 APPROXIMATELY

APPENDIX A

CURRENT VALUE OF GOODS IN BUSINESS

Office Renovations — $654.73:

Furniture:	Office desk	
	4-drawer legal filing cabinet	
	Bookshelf	
	Legal books	
	2 office executive chairs	
	1 steno chair	
	2 computers	
	Plants	
	2 large pictures	
	5 posters	
	2 telephones	
	1 dictaphone machine & recorder	
	1 large oak boardroom table	
	1 executive desk	
	1 table	
	1 radio	
	1 printer	
	1 fax	
		Value: $8,000.00
Vehicle:	20XX Model	Value $3,500.00

APPENDIX B

PROFESSIONAL MEMBERSHIPS

Past Chair	Society for Industrial Security
	Accreditation for Industrial Board
	Association of Security Services
	Advisory Committee on Training
Faculty Member	ABC College
	Education Center
	Learning Institute
Founding Chairperson	Toddler Child Care Association
Active Member	American Association for Security
	Alarm Association
	Fire Protection Association
	Private Investigators Association

3

SALES AND MARKETING

1. Finding Your Brand Identity

Once the decision is made to go into the industry you need to select a name and an identity for your company. This may be one of the most important decisions you make. Your name represents everything about you. One of the oddest choices I ran across was Weasel Security; now does that make you feel safe and secure?

How about Knight Security? That's a nice play on words; knight as in honorable and night as in evening security. Very clever name.

Pinkerton is one of the most renowned names in the industry and was named after its founder Allan Pinkerton. He founded the first private security and detective agency in 1850. The name is solid and represents integrity, knowledge, and history.

Pick a few names that have meanings within the security field and try them out on people; gauge the reactions. It is always nice to recognize people in your family but if you end up with a difficult or meaningless name, it will be a hindrance to your business. Your vision should be clear and the name should reflect that.

2. Your Offering: What Makes You Different?

Now that you have the name down, what makes you different? There are hundreds of thousands of security companies offering anything from a simple mobile patrol to contract services in militarized areas overseas. Where do you fit in and how will you stand out from the crowd?

3. Who Are Your Prospects?

Security is purchased by every single person, whether in the form of motion lights, home alarm systems, guards, store detectives, investigators, bodyguards, or dogs. Every corporation has some form of security. Who are your prospects? When I started in the industry I focused on malls and hotels. Eventually we serviced all the malls and hotels in the Lower Mainland. We provided a look and an image that was wanted at the time: Low-key business attire. From there we grew. Another company started with construction security; it was cheaper to uniform the guards and mostly night work. You start in a market you are familiar with, or you have contacts in, or you have knowledge about.

4. Create a Marketing Plan

Have you developed a marketing plan? This is not as complicated as it sounds; have you figured out a way to get your name in front of the people who purchase your services?

Today, one has to consider in-person sales; social media (various formats); and traditional methods of marketing such as mailouts, networking, newsletters, blogs; the list is almost endless. Start with a plan and revisit it as you go. Change what isn't working, and keep doing what is.

See Sample 12 for an example marketing plan.

5. Advertising and Promotional Materials: Get Your Name out There

You must have a professional image if you want to be taken seriously. Once you've decided on your name and brand image, know that it is not necessary to spend thousands of dollars on an identity. If you can design it yourself, go ahead. Make sure it will work on letterhead, business cards, and online. Most designers today use templates and there are many available to you for free on the Internet. This is money you can use in different ways.

SAMPLE 12
MARKETING PLAN

THE ABC AGENCY
MARKETING PLAN

YEAR 20XX

To provide regular customer awareness of our services the following Marketing procedure will take place:

1. Each year the first mail out will consist of an appropriate introductory letter, brochure, and two business cards.

2. The second mail out will be the picture postcard: "If you need security etc." (The ABC Agency's potential customers.)

3. At Christmas time the top 100 list, all potential clients will receive a specially designed The ABC Agency Christmas card.

In-person Sales Calls: Tape recording of the scurity interview will be left.

Customer Appreciation: Upon completion of a file, the customers will receive a The ABC Agency pen.

Not a designer? Check your local schools for internship students or those who might want to create a design for use in their portfolios for a nominal fee.

You might also consider a brochure or flyer that you can leave with people. All these items mentioned need to tie in together so your company looks professional and trustworthy. See Sample 13.

The following sections cover other advertising and promotional items you need to consider as you launch your business.

5.1 Website

Yes, you need a website. Clients will expect you to have a web presence, especially clients who haven't met you yet and are researching who to call.

What you are starting with will determine how big to go on the site at the start. Today, the choices are enormous. A lot of start-ups use free templates that are Wordpress-based, buy their own domain name (always own your domain name, you don't want someone else to control it), and can either do a simple website themselves or have a decent site developed for less than $500.

The worst websites are those that go on and on and inundate the person with flash and chatter. Make it easy to understand and easy to contact you. I know I lose interest if I have to go through 20 pages to find a contact number or address.

5.2 Newsletter and/or blog

A company newsletter is something your sales and marketing person can develop once you have several staff members, to encourage morale within the company and keep everyone informed. A good newsletter can be modified into a blog on your website that clients can read.

Keep it informative; neither a blog nor a newsletter have to be lengthy, but they have to capture the readers' attention and provide them with some new information. (See Sample 14.)

5.3 Networking

Networking has never gone out of style. You are your company's best salesperson.

Too often I hear company owners saying they don't like to do sales or are not comfortable doing them. Listen: No one can sell your company like you. You know why you are in the business. You know what you can do for someone.

BROCHURE

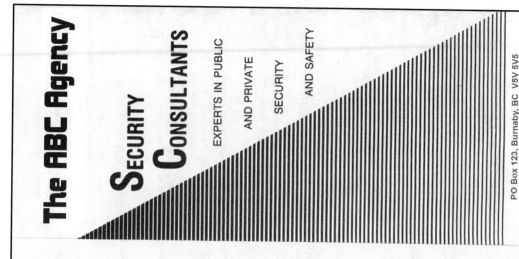

The ABC Agency

SECURITY

CONSULTANTS

EXPERTS IN PUBLIC

AND PRIVATE

SECURITY

AND SAFETY

PO Box 123, Burnaby, BC V5V 5V5
555-555-5555

CLIENTS:

We at The ABC Agency have consulted and conducted programs to more than 80 major organizations during the past ten years. Our clients represent virtually every sector of industry.

References are available from:

FEDERAL GOVERNMENT
PROVINCIAL GOVERNMENT
RETAIL SECTOR
SERVICE INDUSTRIES
TRANSPORTATION
PROPERTY MANAGEMENT
INDUSTRIAL
HOTELS
BANKS
CONSTRUCTION
COMMUNITY COLLEGES
PROFESSIONAL ASSOCIATIONS
RESOURCE-BASED COMPANIES
VOLUNTEER GROUPS

MEMBER OF:

THE SOCIETY FOR INDUSTRIAL SECURITY
AMERICAN SOCIETY FOR SECURITY
CRIME PREVENTION ASSOCIATION
INSTITUTE OF MANAGEMENT

Overview

Since the founding of The ABC Agency in 20XX, we built our reputation on customer service. Our entry into the private security industry was based on providing a variety of stationary and mobile guard services. Over the past few years our focus changed from this area to consultations. **We are not a guard company and do not provide guard services.**

Based on our experience in this field, we are an asset to any organization looking at tender specifications, security instructions, emergency procedures, procedural manuals; determination of the cause or causes of performance problems within an organization, job analysis, organizational development, forcasting, planning, scheduling, budgeting. Additionally we offer a variety of human resource management programs.

The ABC Agency's reputation is based on integrity and credibility. We will assist you in locating the appropriate persons or agencies to solve your problem.

We consult in business, government, health, and education. We work independently or as a project team and will provide high-quality services for your organization.

Services

PROJECT MANAGEMENT

Often the implementation of a security system may span several areas of expertise. The ABC Agency will act as a program coordinator by assisting the clients in determining their needs, selecting the personnel and/or organizations to address those needs, regular client briefings, and troubleshooting problems on the client's behalf. **WE WILL ADDRESS YOUR TECHNOLOGICAL REQUIREMENTS.**

RISK ANALYSIS

Many risks are overlooked or overemphasized. Our analysis entails exposing the risks at hand and assessing the severity, impact, and cost benefit of each.

CRIMINOLOGICAL RESEARCH

Crimes or security problems can be patterned. Similarly, the implementation of a security program may also follow a pattern of its own. The relationship between these two patterns can **IMPACT UPON THE PROFITABILITY OF THE ORGANIZATION.** Proper security measures can be implemented with this knowledge.

ENVIRONMENTAL DESIGN CONSULTANTS

Any physical environment, by it's effect on the movement and actions of people, is either conducive or detrimental to society. Crime Prevention through Environmental Design (CPTED) is a concept that can be applied equally well to environments in the planning stage or already in existence. In many cases simple changes to the physical environment will prevent and deter crime.

MANPOWER — BUDGET PLANNING

The selection of a security service is regularly based solely on the basis of a firm's hourly rates. Although this is certainly a consideration we will work with prospective clients to tailor security systems and programs to their budget.

PROCEDURAL MANUALS

We provide research and formatting, editing to produce quick reference manuals, and/or job specific manuals.
THESE ARE PROPRIETARY TO THE CLIENT

PHYSICAL SECURITY

Our team will meet with you to determine your needs, plan, and design a system that can be tendered to obtain a cost-effective system.

TENDER PREPARATION

Our objective expertise in the security industry allows us to plan and write your security tenders. This ensures your requirements are incorporated and codes and bylaws are met. We will also oversee the tender implementation.

CONTRACT SECURITY

Rates, uniforms, operations management, mobile patrols — we will use our expertise to set up forecasting, planning, scheduling, budgeting, supervisory, and managerial programs that will **DECREASE YOUR COSTS AND INCREASE PROFITS.** Be competitive NOW!

NEWSLETTER GUIDELINES

Employee Newsletter Guidelines

The following format is to be followed in the design of the newsletter. This newsletter is issued with each paycheck to each employee.

Topic 1   **A picture**
Indicating some event that has occurred during the month.

Topic 2   **Sales information**
For example, new contracts, potential clients, and new marketing approach.

Topic 3   **Personnel information**
As in new hires, terminated employees, and any information of the Attorney General that pertains to personnel. Pictures of new employees will also be included in this section.

Topic 4   **Security articles**
Such as items found in Security Magazine items regarding local police, or any helpful information that will help in the performance of security.

Topic 5   **Employee of the month**
A small paragraph pertaining to the person's background and his or her picture will be in this section.

Topic 6   **Editorial comments**
This will be contributions from an employee and outside persons on various security-related topics.

Topic 7   **Educational corner**
I will contribute educational information to each newsletter.

Topic 8   **Personal information**
This will include marriages, moves, births, and events of a similar nature.

Topic 9   **Classified section**
Where people can list items they have for sale, places for rent, or items they are looking for.

Prior to the typing of the newsletter, it is to be edited by the President.

Salespeople are limited in their knowledge of what security guard work is about and often present poorly. Additionally, it can take up to three months to benefit from networking; can you afford to carry a salesperson's wage that long? Start with your own community where you are most likely known. Have you ever volunteered, or coached a children's soccer game? Start with the club. Let them know you have a security business. Get the word out to all your friends and associates. Hand out cards, send emails, and go to chamber meetings. Volunteer to give a talk on a security topic to your rotary club. Provide some free security to a nonprofit group. All of these things get you on the road to having your presence known.

5.4 Referrals

Satisfied clients give referrals to others seeking a similar service. Always provide exemplary service and when finished, ask your clients if they know of three other people who might need a similar service.

Encourage your clients to refer you to others. I send a coffee gift card for every referral I receive.

5.4a Employee referrals

Your employees have their ears at the site. Loyal employees pass on information that they have become privy to at the job. Often they can provide tips on new jobs coming up, or changes in other companies; they have their own network of information. Provide a gift certificate for them as well when they refer other employees or contracts.

5.5 Social media

Social media is a big thing today. People even take courses to learn how to use social media effectively. Unless you have your own marketing department, you need to make it simple.

You can lose hours every day trying to develop a social media following that may or may not increase your sales. Commit yourself to a maximum of 15 minutes a day to get a message across.

Set up a Facebook page and a Twitter account; connect the two of them. Post to one so it automatically updates the other.

Remember that social media is a public forum. Only post informative items; they cannot be site specific as that will breach your client confidentiality concerns. Keep your company Facebook account separate from your personal one. Treat them as two separate entities.

Depending on your knowledge of the Internet you can connect to the other endless communications sites. If this is of no interest to you, look for someone to handle the accounts; just remember if you don't keep on top of what is happening, you will have no idea of how others or particular clients may view your postings. See what your competition is doing and see how it works for them. A lot of people are spending a lot of time posting on social media with minimal results. Weigh the time it takes versus the results.

YouTube videos are an inexpensive and easy way to promote your business. Do a video that instructs a client on how to select a security company; for example, anything that is informative that promotes your business.

5.6 Sales sheets

Incorporate sales sheets into your sales and marketing practices. Keeping track of who you called and when you promised to follow up will maintain your professional image and over time help open doors to new business. There is a sample sales sheet in the download kit included with this book.

OPERATIONS: RUNNING YOUR SECURITY BUSINESS

4

1. Keys to Success in the Security Industry

The first job I ever had in the security industry was as the general manager for a firm that had been started by two men whose lives had been spent working as security officers. They brought to the industry an incredible amount of knowledge in terms of the actual work in the field, but no managerial experience.

In fact my first day on the job involved hiring a clerical person to sort through six large packing boxes full of paper. This was the filing system; each box was labeled with a year and the documents were just thrown in there once the two fellows were finished with them. They were working hard and making no money.

So while we were trying to take control of the paper end in order to establish realistic monthly expenditures and revenues, we were also scheduling people daily. Each day the guards were told to call in to obtain their shift schedules. It was complete chaos, relentless tension and stress, and on a regular basis the phones were cut off because the cash flow was problematic so bills weren't always paid on time.

I had left a job in a related industry where structure, discipline, and record keeping were not only expected but mandatory. These two men had sold me on a great opportunity and although I had no management training at that time I was not afraid of the challenge. I think fear set in the first week — the company operations were barely set up. We put out fire after fire, made little to no progress, and certainly could not plan for change. There was no time with all the crisis management.

I started plotting how our time was spent in the office; five people resolving conflicts and dealing with scheduling problems all day long; training new guards; trying to get uniforms back from people who quit; and dealing with client complaints. It was more than exhausting. However, the industry was fascinating and the potential for growth was obvious.

The starting point for improvements was to deal with client concerns. They always involved guards not showing up on time or knowing what they had to do. Why was this happening? I watched people being hired, given a uniform and a set of keys, and sent to the job site, more often than not that very day. What kind of security was this? Certainly the clients expected and deserved better.

The entire industry was operating in this manner. Untrained guards were working at sites with no clear understanding of what their duties were; clients under the impression they were protected; company managers were flying around at night to get to sites to do on-the-site training; people were quitting after one day or with no notice. It was chaos.

Analysis indicated that there were areas that had to be dealt with immediately to enhance productivity and financial stability. The issues were as follows:

- Employee problems; wrong people hired or sent to wrong locations.

- High turnover; constant staff movement.

- A lack of motivation to perform duties expected.

- Wage reviews were needed.

- Training of staff about the company itself and providing an orientation that included after-hours backup.

- Training of the staff in security itself. At this time security guards in this area required no training of any kind to be licensed; some way of training guards about the site duties that provided consistent service to the client, scheduling in a manner that allowed security staff to plan their lives, and finally motivational strategies to ensure a win-win result for all parties.

I decided the real key to success was that we needed to match the right guard with the client's needs, making sure the guard's work and life needs were met to ensure a commitment to the company for the long term, and reduce costs (when employees left and were unhappy, uniforms were often not returned, people quit on the job, or we lost contracts). There was a potential for an increase in profits if we improved employee morale, motivation, and job performance. It really was a cyclical situation; good employees, superior job performance, happy client, client referrals, word-of-mouth reputation improving, increase in motivated job seekers, great options to meet client requests, and on it goes.

It comes down to a simple equation. Good service given by happy, trained employees = happy customers = more contracts. The following sections describe things to think about in your quest for happy clients and employees.

1.1 What do clients want?

Clients want responsible, properly dressed, courteous, and knowledgeable security staff. They want them to carry out their duties professionally and with minimal interference to their clients, visitors, and business. They want to know their dollar is spent well.

Often, security is a requirement of a business's insurance policy so they feel pressured into maintaining some form of security. Contract security is a less expensive investment for clients since they pay a flat fee for hours worked and do not have to concern themselves with hiring, firing, benefits, and such.

It starts with understanding the needs of the client at a particular job site. The following sections consider what clients want from security staff.

1.1a Image

What image does the client want security to project on their sites? Do they want guards in a police-type uniform? (Make sure to check various legislative restrictions in your area as to what security personnel can and cannot wear and what colors can be used. Chances are they shouldn't look too close to police officers but rules vary according to state/provincial laws.) Do clients prefer guards in business attire such as blazers and slacks?

1.1b Personality

Does the job require excellent communication skills? Does the client expect security to perform a public relations position? Do guards have to answer questions about the building or where particular offices or sections can be found?

Is the job primarily night patrol where observation skills and attention to alarm and locking details is more important than personality?

1.1c Hours

What hours does the client want security to be on site? Will the schedule show 8-hour shifts, over the whole 24 hours? Will they need guards all through the week and on the weekend?

Will they need one or more guards, a mobile patrol, or a dog patrol?

1.2 What do security companies want?

Contract security company owners, like all business owners, want to provide a service and earn a profit. They would like to do this with the least amount of daily disruption and with some assurance that their contracts will be in place each year.

Security companies are the go-betweens for clients and guards.

You'll want to consider the value of each guard and contract in relation to supervisory attendance and problem solving. Are they costing you money or making you money?

1.3 What do guards want?

The majority of guards work in the security field because it interests them. Perhaps they have applied to police forces and enjoy this kind of work, or maybe it is a second job. Often, they are retired and working for some extra money.

Sometimes it is the only job a person can get, and sometimes, he or she really wants to be a professional in the field. The majority of guards seek job security, regular hours, good wages, acknowledgment by management, and respect from clients. Most see training as the foundation for this.

2. Security Contracts

2.1 Contract start-up

There are many things to think about when starting work on a new contract, including:

- When does each contract start?

- Are you moving staff from other sites to maintain your company image and level of service? Will you use a combination of staff, old and new? How many staff are required? Do more staff have to be hired?

- Which supervisor's area will the contract fall under?

- Will the site order book? Will information be ready for the first day of work? Does the office have the required operational binders and standing orders ready to go to the site?

- Who is meeting with the client representative to review the job requirements and have the site orders (post orders) approved by the client?

- Is there enough time to have the information sheet and contract signed and all arrangements in place before the contract starts?

- Has operations been informed of the new job so they can add the information to their scheduling board?

- Has the site been given a code name for internal "on air" communications?

If a company has planned properly, the procedural flow becomes automatic:

1. New contract is obtained.

2. Administration:
    - Assigns a contract number and forwards information to operations and accounting.
    - Prepares appropriate contract and diarizes due date for return, forwards contract to client, advises management, and follows through for completion.

3. Accounting:
    - Enters new site information on accounting program and assigns project reference to track profit and loss on a monthly basis.

4. Human Resources:
    - Provided with client expectations for staff, and reviews current staff to determine who should work at the site or whether new staff are required.

- Pulls employee information for operations and makes recommendations.
- Schedules orientation sessions for new staff.

5. Operations:
   - Enters scheduling information.
   - Makes final decision as to staffing.
   - Assigns staff — full-time/part-time as required.
   - Prepares, reviews site orders, and ensures operational binder is on site.
   - Assigns supervisor to be accountable for site.
   - Talks to scheduled staff and provides them with schedule.
   - Provides schedule to client.

6. Management:
   - Confers with client.
   - Obtains signed contract.
   - Monitors staffing/scheduling to meet needs of client prior to contract starting.
   - Ensures communication with client is on a regular basis.

2.2 Sample contract

Here is a sample letter and contract that I have used in my agency in Sample 15. It is important to remember that you must have your contract reviewed by your legal counsel to ensure that you are covering all local and state or provincial (where applicable) requirements and terms.

3. Reporting and Rules

3.1 Site binder

Located at each site is the post order binder, which contains all the information and forms required to successfully complete the required duties. Included within the binder are several sections as explained below:

- Schedules: The current monthly schedule provides a breakdown of hours of work, name of scheduled guard, and the duration of shift for each day of the month.

CONTRACT AND LETTER

The ABC Agency
123 Main Street
Burnaby, BC
V5V 5V5

Date: March 1, 20XX

Dear Client:

Re: Contract #

Attached, please find two copies of your contract with The ABC Agency.

If you find the terms of this agreement acceptable, please sign and attached your corporate seal on both copies of the contract.

Return one copy of the contract with Completed Post Orders to our attention and retain the other copy with the Completed Post Orders for your records.

If you have any questions about this contract, please do not hesitate to contact us.

Your sincerely,

Bob Smith
President
The ABC Agency

DATED the 1st of March, 20XX.

BETWEEN:

    The ABC Agency

                  OF THE FIRST PART

AND:

    Joe Client

                  OF THE SECOND PART

AGREEMENT

THIS AGREEMENT made the ___1___ day of ___March___ 20XX.

BETWEEN:

> The ABC Agency, a body corporate, having a place of business at 123 Main Street, Burnaby, British Columbia V5V 5V5;
>
> (hereinafter called the "Security Service")

OF THE FIRST PART

AND   Joe Client

> (hereinafter called the "Company")

OF THE SECOND PART

> WITNESSETH that in consideration of the mutual covenants hereinafter set forth, the parties hereto, on behalf of themselves, their successors and assigns, covenant and agree as follows:

1. The Security Service agrees to supply at the Company's premises located at _____ security guards to perform the duties requested by the Company as set out in the Security Standing Orders, a copy of which has been signed by the parties hereto and is annexed hereto as Schedule "A."

2. The Company during the period from _____, 20XX to _____, 20XX, being the term of this Agreement, agrees to pay the Security Service for the services of each security guard in accordance with the following table:

Regular Hours Rate	$
Overtime Hourly Rate	$
Statutory Holiday Rate	$
Guard Dog Hourly Rate	$
Mobile Patrol Rate	$

3. Should the Company require any additional shifts for special events and/or hours over and above those set out in Schedule "A," or extra duties, then the Company agrees to pay the Security Service for the services of each security guard in accordance with the following table:

Regular Hours Rate	$
Overtime Hourly Rate	$
Statutory Holiday Rate	$
Guard Dog Hourly Rate	$
Mobile Patrol Rate	$

4. The Security Service shall submit its accounts from its time sheets covering a one- (1) month period. Payment shall be made to the Security Service at 123 Main Street, Burnaby, British Columbia, V5V 5V5 within ten (10) days after the receipt of the accounts by the Company.

5. The Company shall pay to the Security Service interest on outstanding accounts at the rate of eighteen percent (18%) per annum calculated and compounded monthly.

6. The Security Guards shall remain employees of the Security Service which shall be solely responsible for the arrangements of reliefs and substitutions, pay, supervision, discipline, employment insurance, Workers' Compensation, leave, uniforms, and all other matters arising out of the relationships between employer and employee.

7. The Security Service agrees to indemnify and save the Company harmless from any costs, claims, demands, suits, actions, or judgments made, brought or recovered against the Company resulting from any negligent act of omission by the Security Service or its employees in connection with the services covered by this Agreement.

8. The Company agrees to indemnify and save the Security Service and its employees harmless from any loss, costs, claims, charges, suits, actions, or judgments made, brought, or recovered against the Security Services or any of its employees resulting from their performance of any of the duties set forth in this Agreement in the Security Standing orders or any amendment thereto, or the carrying out by any such employee of any instructions given to him or her by any official of the Company.

9. This Agreement may be terminated at the end of any pay period by either party upon thirty (30) days' written notice.

10. The Company agrees that it will not, for a period of one (1) year after the ter-mination of this Agreement or any extension or renewal thereof, employ in any capacity whatsoever any person who as an employee of the Security

Service has been engaged in guard duty at the Company's premises, and that it will not knowingly enter into any contract for guard duty with any other person, firm, or corporation under which guards formerly employed by the Security Services are assigned to duty at the Company's premises.

11. The failure of either party at any time to require performance by the other party of any provision hereof shall in no way affect the full right to require such performance at any time thereafter; nor shall a waiver by either party of any breach of the provisions hereof be taken or held to be a waiver of any succeeding breach of such provisions or as a waiver of the provision itself.

12. This Agreement constitutes the entire agreement between the parties and supersedes all previous agreements and understandings between the parties in any way relating to the subject matter hereof. It is expressly understood and agreed that the Security Service has made no representations, inducements, warranties, or promises whether direct, indirect, or collateral, oral or otherwise, concerning this Agreement, the matters herein, the services to be provided hereunder, or concerning any other matters which are not embodied herein.

13. If the Security service shall not have received notice from the Company at least thirty (30) days prior to the expiration of the term of this Agreement without the execution and delivery of a new Agreement or a written renewal or extension of this Agreement, there will be deemed to be an extension of this Agreement on a month-to-month basis upon the same terms and conditions as set forth is this Agreement, so far as applicable.

14. All notices, requests, demands, or other communications (hereinafter collectively called "Notices") by the terms hereof required or permitted to be given by one party to another shall be given in writing by personal delivery or by registered mail, postage prepaid, addressed to the other party or delivered to such other party as follows:

   a. To the Security Service at:

      123 Main Street
      Burnaby, British Columbia
      V5V 5V5

   b. To the Company at:

      _____
      _____
      _____

or at such other address as may be given by one of them to the other in writing from time to time, and such Notices shall be deemed to have been received when delivered, or if mailed, forty-eight (48) hours after 12:01 a.m. on the date of the mailing thereof, provided that if such Notices shall have been mailed and if regular mail service shall be interrupted by a strike or other irregularity before the deemed receipt of such Notices as aforesaid, then such Notices shall not be effective unless delivered.

IN WITNESS WHEREOF the parties hereto have executed these presents on the day and year first above written.

THE COMMON SEAL OF   )
The ABC Agency   )
was hereunto affixed in   )
the presence of:)
)
)
)
_____   )
)
)
_____   )
)
)
)
THE COMMON SEAL OF   )
)
Joe Client   )
)
was hereunto affixed in the presence of:)
)
_____   )
)
_____   )
)

- Report Sheets/Incident Reports: Blank storage of forms that must be completed. Report Sheets are to be completed for each posted shift worked and will account for time, duties performed, and times of call-in's as they apply at each site. Refer to the post orders for specific reporting requirements.

- Incident Logs: These are to be completed each time you take action other than what is normally required such as when requested to assist; contacting a reference; and advised of a criminal, medical, or fire situation. This report will cover all actions taken, a complete description of the problem, and any resolution to the problem or situation. Extensive reports may require the use of a regular report sheet to be used as a second page. In this case, ensure the pages are numbered and securely attached.

- Site Log: The site log is divided into two categories to assist in locating specific information.

- Procedures and Problems: This is an ongoing message book that assists in assuring all guards receive the same information. Constant review will ensure that you have the most recent instructions. Complete each part of the log as below, in a professional manner and limiting use to relative subjects.

- Identifications: For descriptions of individuals and particular instructions as to handling them. Entries may be made due to a threat or disturbance or due to unusual activity and are included in order that all guards be aware of these individual's presence. Complete each part with the description and instruction. Refer to the location and availability of further information.

- Memos: Memos to guards from the client should be placed in this section for review of lengthy procedure instructions or events to take place, that are not contained within the post orders. At some sites, these may be divided into two parts — temporary or permanent memos.

- Post Orders: The Post orders are the specific instructions as to how to perform your regular guard duties. They are usually indexed and will provide for all eventualities. You are to be familiar with all aspects of the post orders. Some sites may have post orders and emergency procedures in separate categories.

- Permanent Orders: These orders are set out in a manual that set the standard procedures and instructions for all guards irrespective of building or location for the company or agency. They also set out the deportment, dress, and conduct required of all the guards employed. Generally they are the last item in the site binder. The Canadian Society of Industrial Security recommends using certain guidelines for setting up post orders, discussed in the next section.

3.2 Site/post orders

At the core of the industry are site/post orders. They are the instructions that the client wants followed at his or her location (also known as a site or post). Post orders are the specific instructions as to how to perform the regular guard duties. They are usually indexed and will provide for all eventualities.

It is important for guards to be familiar with all aspects of the post orders. Some sites may have post orders and emergency procedures in separate categories. These are the most important documents for a company or organization with contract guards; they must be clear, concise, current, and complete. These orders outline in detail what is expected of the guards at that site by management. This eliminates the obvious problems associated with word-of-mouth instructions.

By referring to a site binder that should be at each site, a new guard can handle most emergency situations after reviewing the instructions; it also allows for providing temporary coverage in case of illness with minimal disruption to the client site.

When writing post orders remember the following rules:

1. Set up a site binder for each site that is divided into easy-to-use and relevant sections that will hold post orders.

2. Write in basic language.

3. Maintain dates on each page so updated information can be inserted as required.

4. Maintain a signature sheet to ensure that all guards on site are informed and acknowledge review of updated information.

See Samples 16 and 17.

3.2a Post Order Format

Use a simple and standardized layout for your post orders.

1. Input your post orders on the computer and assign a name and date for them.

2. Ensure your headings stand out.

POST ORDER REVIEW

Post Order Review

Job Site: _____

Date	Comments	Guard # and Initials

SAMPLE 17
POST ORDERS MASTER

Post Orders Master

Site: _____

PO In for Typing	Out to Client — Approval	Received from Client	Issued to Site	Issued to On-Call	Issued to Mobile

3. Make instructions concise and understandable; use pictures where necessary.

4. When you amend pages ensure you update the date and ensure it is not on the log so that oncoming staff are aware of a change.

5. Ensure changes to the clients callout and emergency numbers are updated immediately and via email to your company.

POST ORDER FORMAT

The first page should contain the following information:

TITLE — POST ORDERS
NAME OF BUILDING
ADDRESS OF BUILDING
PREPARED BY
DATE:

Signing Authorities
    Position
    Place and Date

The second page should contain:

    INDEX

        A complete and concise index together with cross-references where required.

The third page should contain:

    EMERGENCY PHONE NUMBERS

    These should include the following:

        POLICE:

        FIRE:

        AMBULANCE

        HOSPITAL:

        MAINTENANCE:

        HEATING:

        ELECTRICAL:

        ALARM COMPANY:

        ELEVATOR REPAIR PERSON:

        DEPARTMENTAL or COMPANY REPRESENTATIVES: To be contacted in the event or emergency.

(These numbers should be office, cell phone, and home phone numbers.)

The fourth page commences the actual instructions to the guard:

AS TO WHAT IS REQUIRED AT THE POST:

1. INTRODUCTION

These orders should be read in conjunction with Permanent Orders and where there is a conflict, Permanent Orders will take precedence.

The guard should familiarize himself or herself with all orders and instruction.

2. SITE SHIFT COVERAGE

This should give hours of duty for each guard at this post.

Example:

2400–0800 1 guard

0800–1600 1 guard

1600–1200 2 guards (guard number 2 to patrol and supervise cleaning staff)

Guard should report at least ten minutes prior to commencement of shift for any instruction or information from outgoing guard.

It is easiest to post your site schedule here and when changes are made a new one can be emailed to the site.

3. LOCATION OF POST

Details as to the exact location of the guards post and whether it is stationary or mobile.

4. DUTIES OF GUARD

Describe the duties expected of the guard at this post in general and note the specifics under the separate headings under this section. Make sure you cover the following points for each site.

a. Reporting

Many Workers' Compensation requirements involve hourly reporting to a supervisor or call central. Ensure this is outlined and the times it is to take place. This is for the safety of the security guard.

b. Patrols

Indicate the times patrols are to be made, whether regular rounds or staggered, whether a punch clock is used or any type of recording system, what route should be used or varied, what items are to be looked for while on patrol. Attach any maps with specific details here.

c. Locking and Unlocking Doors

Indicate a complete list of doors and when they should be locked and unlocked. A building plan map should be inserted here.

d. Keys

Indicate the general instructions for the guard regarding keys at the post. Attach specific key instructions here.

e. Cleaning Staff

This should give the hours cleaning is done, the name of the company and contact at the company should there be a problem, including office and home telephone number.

Also included here should be any area where cleaning staff are restricted and if they have to be under escort.

f. Building Passes

Outline the guard's duties in relation to permanent passes or temporary passes. Ensure there are pictures of same to double check. Ensure client communication of changes is recorded in the post order book for daily review by the various shifts.

g. Access Control

Detailed instructions as to who is to be allowed in to the building and whether personnel have integrated access cards is required. It should also include —

1. whether or not employees have to show passes;

2. when employees are required to sign in and out, if this is applicable;

3. description of form to use for signing in both visitors and employees working after hours.

h. Visitors

This should be specific instructions of what procedure to follow regarding visitors; for example, free entry, signing in, escorts, etc.

i. Fire

Detailed list of who the guard is expected to call other than the fire department; in this instance, it may include company and client management.

j. Bomb Threat or Threatening Phone Calls

This is not an uncommon issue for guards in high public-traffic areas. In fact, specialized training is a consideration for security staff. Nevertheless ensure you outline the procedures the client wants taken in these situations.

k. Injury to Personnel

List instructions for guard in the event of an injury to employees. Are the security guards trained in first-aid and expected to provide it? If not, what procedure does the client want done?

l. Electrical Power Failure

Instructions on what to do in the event of failure including contacts and if there is auxiliary power, any instructions.

m. Heat Loss or Other Emergencies

Indicate specific procedures to follow in each emergency.

n. Lost and Found

Where items are located provide instructions to the guard for the disposition of lost and found articles.

o. Removal of Material and/or Equipment by Employees

Familiarize the guard who notices employees or other persons removing equipment and material from the building with what they are expected to do and whether they require written authority.

p. Reports and Reporting Procedures

Provide the client requirements for shift reports, incident logs, and such.

q. Telephones

Provide instruction to the guard how phones should be answered; for example, "Good morning, Department Security Desk."

r. Parking

If there is parking on the premises, instructions regarding illegal parking, etc.

s. Accidents

What are the instructions in case of an accident? This is especially important on constructions sites (e.g., who to notify, phone numbers).

t. Press, Radio, Photographers

Clear instructions as to how to deal with press, radio, and photographers; who to call, access to site, and so on.

u. Notebooks

Instructions for completing notebooks and disposition of the same.

v. Peddlers and Canvassers

Instructions as to who is allowed or not allowed on site.

w. Newspapers and Messengers

x. Designated Authorities

4. Standing Orders or Permanent Orders

Standing or permanent orders can be as short or as detailed as the company wants. The idea behind them is that regardless of where the guard is working, company policies and procedures are outlined for reference or review purposes.

Standing orders cover the following company rules and regulations which would include such topics as:

- Conduct of guards while on duty
- Deportment
- Procedural process
- Company flow chart
- Reporting expectations
- Incident management
- Police and public relations
- Accident procedure and reporting requirements
- Workers' safety reporting requirements
- Fire protection procedures
- Handling aggressive or intoxicated persons
- Basic criminal code sections

Let's review some operational issues that require standing order implementation prior to starting.

5. Reports and Incidents

Do you have a report or an incident form ready to go? Here is a simple template for all stationary guards to complete each shift in Sample 18.

Incident reports are to be completed for anything out of the ordinary that may require further action by management or is strictly information for security and client management. Numbering incident reports makes them easier to find and review later. Supply each post-order book with at least 20 numbered reports.

Reports are either collected or emailed nightly along with incidents. This allows management to troubleshoot and preempt client calls.

See Sample 19.

REPORT SHEET

Report Sheet

Date: _____   Guard: _____

Location: _____   Shift: _____

Time		Call In

6. Keys and Alarms

Often, security must maintain a set of master keys for each building. Control of these keys must be recorded. We have provided you with a series of forms that can assist in this process; a key log, a key control list, and a fire alarms information notice in Samples 20, 21, and 22. Control of keys and alarms are standard requirements on most jobs.

7. Mobile Patrols

One way to reduce costs and plan routes and monitor patrol activities is a GPS tracker. This is a common tool used by many companies that provide company vehicles. Today there are so many easy ways to plan routes — Google Earth, Google Maps, MapQuest — that can save you thousands of dollars in misspent hours and wages.

Mobile patrols are only cost-effective if you plan the routes carefully. Have you determined the routes for any mobile patrols to take?

A run sheet such as the one shown in Sample 23 will help you determine the route in relation to costs involved in operating a mobile detail.

Over the years we found it necessary to have staff sign a mobile patrol release form to cover ourselves legally. This may or may not be allowed in your area but it is worth checking with your legal advisors. I have included a sample in the download kit that came with this book.

Sample 24 shows you how to keep track of alert information for your mobile. This keeps track of changes, who made them, and can provide you an easy log when communicating with your client or when there is a conflict.

Will you use your mobile patrol as a supervisory position? If yes, then you will want to have a supervisory patrol sheet. See Sample 25.

A series of inquiries will need to be made in order to develop post orders for each mobile site: property references, vacant premises reports, emergency procedures sheets, and more. Find all these helpful forms in the download kit.

8. Scheduling

I have always found it amazing that scheduling staff in a logical, considerate manner can be so problematic. When all is said and done, scheduling is a mathematical issue. Once you know how many hours

INCIDENT REPORT

INCIDENT REPORT

Date: _____

Time: _____

Guard Reporting: _____

Location: _____

Incident: _____

_____

_____

_____

_____

_____

Complainant's Name: _____

Address: _____

Phone: _____

Action Taken: _____

Follow-up: _____

Were Police Contacted?: _____

Time of Arrival: _____

Time of Departure: _____

Police File No.: _____

Name: _____

Supervisor Contacted: _____

Time: _____

Management Comments: _____

_____

_____

_____

_____

_____

Reviewed By: _____

SAMPLE 20
KEY LOG

Key Log

Date Issued	Guard Name & No.	Date Recorded	Comments

Date Opened: _____

Site: _____

Client: _____

Code Name: _____

Total Sets Received:

Sets consist of: _____   _____

                        _____   _____

                        _____   _____

                        _____   _____

                        _____   _____

Set Issued to Guard: _____   _____

                        _____   _____

                        _____   _____

                        _____   _____

Set Issued to Mobile: _____   _____

                        _____   _____

                        _____   _____

                        _____   _____

Set Issued to Oncall: _____   _____

                        _____   _____

                        _____   _____

                        _____   _____

Other Comments: _____

_____

_____

_____

_____

_____

SAMPLE 21
KEY CONTROL LIST

Key Control List

Date	Key Type	Issued To	Signature	Returned	Signature

FIRE ALARM NOTICE

[Insert Company Letterhead]

DATE _____

Dear Client:

Please complete the following fire information form and leave it on your desk for mobile patrol to pick up. This information will greatly assist our mobile patrol in dealing with any fire situations in your building.

1) Do you wish [Company Name] to answer fire alarms for your building? If so, please answer the following questions;

2) Do you expect [Company Name] to silence the alarm? [ ] Yes [ ] No

3) Do you expect [Company Name] to reset the alarm? [ ] Yes [ ] No

4) Does [Company Name] have access to the fire panel? [ ] Yes [ ] No

5) Where is the fire panel located? _____

6) Where is the key to the fire panel located? _____

7) Where are the silence/reset buttons? _____

8) Who monitors the alarm? _____

9) What is the monitoring service's phone number? _____

10) Does the monitoring service have our name and phone number?
    [ ] Yes   [ ] No

11) Will the monitoring service:
    [ ] Call the building reference, OR
    [ ] Leave it to [Company Name]'s discretion?

Thank you for your time and attention to this matter.

Sincerely yours,

[Company Name]

MOBILE RUN SHEET

Mobile Run Sheet

Mileage out: _____   Date: _____

Mileage in: _____   Driver: _____

Total Mileage: _____   Vehicle: _____

Gas Oil   Brake Fluid   Electrical/Mechanical Problems   Body & Tire Damage

_____

_____

_____

Site & Code Name	In	Out	In	Out	In	Out	In	Out	In	Out	In	Out

Time:	

SAMPLE 24
MOBILE PATROL LOG BOOK

Mobile Patrol Log Book

Date	Written By	Information	Comments

MOBILE FIELD SUPERVISOR RUN SHEET

**Mobile Field Supervisor
Run Sheet**

Date: _____

Field Supervisor: _____   Shift: _____

Vehicle: Company   [ ]   Mileage: Out _____   In _____   Total _____

Other   [ ]   Mileage: Total _____

Sites	Guard(s)	Time In	Time Out

Fuel Expense $ _____   Quantity _____

Company Credit Card   [ ]   Attach receipt to this report

Other   [ ]   Attach receipt to this report

Additional Information

Additional Information

Time	

you need and where the hours are to be distributed, you simply figure out how many staff you need.

For example, take a site with a need for 56 hours of coverage. In British Columbia, 40 hours is a full-time work week for guards. So 56 hours would equal one full-time person and one part-time person. If the hours needed would be, say, Monday to Friday, 16:00 to 24:00 hours (since we use the 24-hour clock in this industry), and Saturday and Sunday 08:00 to 16:00 hours. you would focus on one regular person during the week, and the part-time weekend hours are perfect for a student.

The key to scheduling is to match the guard to the site so you can keep him or her there long term with a trained backup available. Let's say the job requirements are Monday to Friday afternoon shift. Find a guard who wants these hours; perhaps it is someone who goes to school during the day and wants a regular evening job, or perhaps it is a retired person earning a second income. Whomever you find that matches this criteria, work with him or her. The worst decision is to place someone into that job who has a completely opposite lifestyle requirement (i.e., a mother who wants to be home with her children at night).

Remember, if a person wants full-time work and you only give him or her part-time work, you will lose the person. If a person only wants part-time and you keep scheduling him or her for full-time, he or she eventually quit. The scheduling person gets to know the staff and what they are capable of doing.

Mrs. Personality? Put her where the client wants a friendly, chatty security guard at the door. If your client has a secure facility that wants a guard to look the part and do enforcement only, choose your employee specifically for this position.

It is important that your staff get rest, too, or when you need people for a special event, they simply will not be available. Don't overwork them.

Whether you use the old-fashioned wall-scheduling board or a computerized program, the goal is stability. The more stability you have with staff and client satisfaction, the less your operations become a crisis-management center. Burnout is a serious problem in operations. Plan, prepare, and prevent problems.

5

HUMAN RESOURCES

Security companies' largest staffing expenditure is generally due to the operations department. Without clearly defining the objectives of each job and ensuring a client-guard match occurs, turnover is high. However, if you are following the concepts discussed in this book, you can minimize impact.

Smaller guard companies need driven, motivated staff to help them grow; larger companies want to recruit top-notch personnel as people move into more involved roles, investigative positions, management, and so on.

1. Recruiting

How will you recruit new security guards? Employers often post listings on Craigslist. This will bring in hundreds of applications and provide you with hours of screening time.

Security employees tend to move around a fair bit until they land a position where the wages and hours are reasonable, so recruiting becomes a long, involved process wherein either the owner or the personnel manager must be clear on what his or her immediate goals are. Is the job an evening position where door access is a primary concern and after about 8:00 p.m. there is little to do? Then perhaps a retired person looking for a second income will be your most reliable employee.

Write your employee ads in such a way that they attract the person you are looking for. If need be, write more than one for different positions.

2. Hiring

Hiring the right staff is the most critical part of human resources. I recall working for a company where it put the president's daughter into the position of human resources manager and she was 19. Soon it became obvious that all the new guards were attractive young men, and while they were nice to look at, they did not always fit the jobs we were trying to fill.

Having applicants fill out an application form that asks enough questions you can verify along with them submitting a résumé is the way to go.

Sample 26 is a sample application form that can be used and asks detailed questions about the person's work history.

Too often people are hired today without any verification of the statements made on their application forms. I recommend checking and verifying the information prior to interviewing the person. I have had many discussion and disagreements with people on this issue but the bottom line is: Why interview someone that has lied on his or her application form or had his or her employers provide you with different reasons for terminations than the employee gave? This seems to me a waste of time. Manage your time by ensuring you are only interviewing those people that warrant it and do verification and reference checks before interviews.

Due to privacy issues, employers are often reluctant to provide information without a written request. This can be done in letter form and faxed or emailed to the previous employer (see Sample 27).

I cannot overstate the amount of applications I have received that were not honest. In fact, in one case, the woman had completely invented her background. Perhaps she was used to having no one check the legitimacy of her work history.

There are also tests available today that you can purchase for a very small amount of money that will provide an assessment of the potential employee. This might be a consideration when hiring supervisory or managerial staff There are a variety offered on the Internet by various organizations — look for integrity tests.

SAMPLE 26
APPLICATION FOR EMPLOYMENT

APPLICATION FOR EMPLOYMENT

Date: _____

Name: _____
        Last   First   Middle

Address: _____

Postal Code: _____

Phone #: _____

Date of Birth: _____

SSN/SIN: _____

Driver's Lic. #: _____ Height: _____ Weight: _____ Eye color: _____

State or Prov. of Issue _____ Do you own a vehicle? Yes [ ] No [ ]

Place of residence for past ten years (From most recent to least recent)

Street, Apt. # _____ City or Town _____ From – To _____

_____

_____

_____

_____

_____

Present Citizenship: _____

Name of Next of Kin: _____ Relationship to you: _____

Address of Next of Kin: _____

_____

Phone # of Next of Kin: _____

Education

Last Grade Completed: _____ Year: _____

Postsecondary Diploma or Degree: _____

_____

FOR OFFICE USE ONLY

Date of Hire: _____

Employee #: _____

Badge #: _____

TD1 Claim ($): _____

F.D.W.: _____

L.D.W.: _____

Other Training: _____

_____

_____

_____

Hobbies: _____

_____

Have you ever been convicted of a criminal offense? _____

If yes, give the nature of offense, date, and place in space provided below:

_____

_____

_____

Are you applying for **full-time employment** [   ] or **part-time** [   ]?

Are you willing to relocate?   Yes [   ] No [   ]

If yes, to what area would you like to relocate? _____

Personal References (Local preferred, no relatives):

1) Name: _____   Position: _____

   Address: _____   Phone: _____

   How long have you known this person? _____

2) Name: _____   Position: _____

   Address: _____   Phone: _____

   How long have you known this person? _____

3) Name: _____   Position: _____

   Address: _____   Phone: _____

   How long have you known this person? _____

Employment history for the past ten years (from the most recent to the least recent)

1) Company Name: _____   Type of Business: _____

   Address:_____   From: _____ To: _____

   Job Title: _____   Duties Performed: _____

   Reason for Leaving: _____

2) Company Name: _____ Type of Business: _____

    Address:_____ From: _____ To:_____

    Job Title: _____ Duties Performed: _____

Reason for Leaving:_____

3) Company Name: _____ Type of Business: _____

    Address:_____ From: _____ To:_____

    Job Title: _____ Duties Performed: _____

Reason for Leaving:_____

Please use the following area for any further information you wish to add or did not have room for on the previous page.

_____

_____

_____

_____

I hereby certify that <u>ALL</u> information given is true and correct. I hereby grant [Company Name] <u>FULL</u> permission to make all necessary enquiries concerning my character, finances, and qualifications. I further understand that any false statement made on this application may result in immediate termination of my employment should I become an employee of [Company Name.]

Note: I hereby understand that as an employee of [Company Name] I must be approved for Fidelity Bonding. Should bonding not be granted, my position will be immediately terminated. I am in agreement with the terms of this employment.

_____

Signature of Applicant

SAMPLE 27
REFERENCE CHECK

DATE: _____

Dear Fellow Employer:

RE: _____

The above-named person has applied for a position with our firm as a Security Guard. Would you kindly complete the following information to aid in our character investigation? Thank you for your time and attention to this matter.

1. Date of Employment: FROM _____ TO _____

2. You consider his or her past work performance to be —

    a. Excellent   [   ]
    b. Good   [   ]
    c. Below Average   [   ]
    d. Poor   [   ]
    e. No Comment   [   ]

3. Was the employee punctual?   Yes [   ] No [   ]

4. Were there any drug- or alcohol-related problems with
   this person?   Yes [   ] No [   ]

5. Did this employee work cooperatively with other employees?   Yes [   ] No [   ]

6. Would you rehire this person?   Yes [   ] No [   ]

7. Further comments: _____
   _____
   _____
   _____
   _____

Once again, thank you for your consideration in completing this form. Please do not hesitate to call our office should you have any inquiries.

Sincerely yours,

Personnel Department
   [Company Name]

I think today that politeness and courtesy are often overlooked due to time pressures and the need to be immediately accessible. Nevertheless I think it is imperative that you advise a person when he or she is not being considered. Sample 28 is a sample rejection letter that can easily be formatted on your computer and emailed to applicants.

Whenever you hire someone, provide him or her with a job description. Sample 29 is a sample of a generic one.

Sounds silly, right? I mean, after all, everyone knows what a security guard does! Well, not really, and sometimes not even the guard fully understands the expectations. Security is an industry that often lacks training. Provide employees with a clear description of what the company expects. Give them a copy and have them sign a copy for their personnel file.

The next thing to provide is the Employee Orientation Handbook; read more on training in Chapter 6.

3. Uniforms

Before you decide on a uniform strategy, check the laws in your area. For instance, if you provide uniforms, you can require employees wear a certain color of shoe and the employee is responsible for purchasing the shoes. Specific additional items may include flashlights but most security guards come equipped with their own and their own cell phones — which have replaced cameras in most instances.

One of the companies I worked for was unionized and the contract stipulated that shirts did not have to be returned at the end of employment. If that employment lasted only one day, the uniform costs were enormous. Some companies set up a payroll deduction system that have the employee pay for the actual costs of his or her uniform over a series of pay dates, and then the uniform would be returned at the end of employment and, based on its condition, a full or partial refund was made to the employee. Inventory control became an issue and over a period of time we came up with different strategies.

The first strategy was to carry all the uniform supplies with the logo placed on all the shirts, blazers, and parkas. But there was always a sizing problem with pants and shirts.

The second strategy was limiting the logo to blazers and parkas.

The third strategy and most cost-effective was to issue a chit to the new employee where he or she went to the supplier and were outfitted

SAMPLE 28
REJECTION LETTER

[Insert Company Letterhead]

Date:

Dear Applicant:

Thank you for submitting an application to [Company Name]. Regretfully, we do not have any openings available for you at this time.

We will keep your application on file and should anything become available that meets your qualifications we will be in touch with you.

Once again, thank you for your interest in our firm.

Sincerely yours,

Personnel Department

JOB DESCRIPTION

[Company Name]
JOB DESCRIPTION

Accountable to the Operations Manager or Site Supervisor, if one is designated. Responsible for:

1. Protection of physical and human resources at sites assigned.

2. Performance of all regular and special patrol functions in accordance with Post Orders.

3. Ensuring, prior to commencement to shift:

   a. Uniform is neat and clean and conforms to regulations as prescribed by the [Insert relevant Acts and company names].

   b. Operable pen, notepad, and security license are carried.

   c. That other designated equipment is carried, such as two-way radios and pagers.

4. Being familiar with, and reviewing periodically, all Post Orders, Company Regulations, Standing Orders, and Special Directives for site.

5. Completing for each shift worked all Report Sheets, Incident Logs, and other documentations as required.

6. Undertaking, as a condition of Employment, renew all internal and external security training courses, as required by the Operations Manager.

7. Attending all staff meetings.

8. Reporting to the Operations Manager or Site Supervisor any action, condition, or special problems which could endanger security staff or violate conditions of work.

with properly sized pants and shirts and we were invoiced for them. We provided them with the exterior clothing directly from our racks. The only time this system did not work well was for emergency callout work where new staff had to be hired to go to work immediately. We always kept a small supply of shirts and pants in the most common sizes for men and women.

We maintained strict control over uniforms and had every employee sign a form acknowledging what they had received.

Sample 31 is an inventory form that you can modify for your organization (also available in the download kit).

4. General Human Resources Records and Administration

Records management is an important part of the human resources department. I recommend two files for every employee: a personnel file and a payroll file.

The personnel file should maintain a certain information flow (see Sample 32). This sheet was kept on the left side of the file folder and was maintained by human resources. It allows for a quick review of all the information in an employee's file and, certainly in union environments, provides your backup documentation.

Once the employee leaves your employ or is terminated, an Employee Termination Form can be completed and the file closed. Sample 33 ensures the correct information is recorded about the employee at the time of termination and all future administrators will be able to answer reference questions correctly.

5. Employee Supervision

Proper supervision and evaluation of security personnel is required to maintain effective operations. Our company structure had mobile officers appointed as supervisors and one of their regular duties was to drop into their allocated sites and do random spot-checks. They were required to complete a form and leave it for management to review in the morning (see Sample 34).

Duties are clearly outlined in this job description for an area supervisor in Sample 34.

This form was provided to operations, which would forward it to personnel.

UNIFORM CONTRACT

Uniform Contract

Date: _____   Name: _____

Employee No.: _____   Badge No.:_____

[Company Name] agrees to provide to the employee uniform items as per this agreement. In return, the employee agrees as follows:

a) Not to wear any portion of the uniform except when on duty or when en route to and from the job site.

b) Upon termination of employment, the employee agrees to return all items of clothing and equipment to [Company Name] or a cash equivalent thereof. This includes the security license and/or any other identification issued.

c) Before a terminated employee will receive his or her final pay, all items issued must be turned in to the office dry-cleaned and neatly packaged.

d) The cost of the uniform will be deducted over a two-month period.

e) Required to wear a <u>complete uniform</u> at all times during a scheduled shift.

I HAVE READ AND FULLY UNDERSTAND THE ABOVE AND AGREE TO THE ABOVE MENTIONED CONDITIONS.

_____
EMPLOYEE SIGNATURE

_____
ISSUED BY

Item	Qty	Size	Date Issued	Initial	Date Returned	Returned/ Replaced — Reason
Blazer (F)						
Blazer (M)						
Blouse						
Shirts						
Culottes						
Slacks						
Coveralls						
Mobile Jacket						
Parka						
Raincoat						
Sweater						
Tie (F)						
Tie (M)						
Sec. Emp. License						
Flashes						
Card						
Tag						

*Cost of missing items to be paid by employees.

SAMPLE 31
MONTHLY INVENTORY REPORT

Monthly Inventory Report

Stationary _____

Site/Goods _____

Uniforms _____

From: _____

Date _____

For Month of: _____

Item	Minimum Constant	In Stock	Required
Post Order Binder	5		
Flashlight	5		
Batteries	5		
Report Sheets	500		
Incident Logs	200		
Window Stickers	50		
Metal Signs	10		
Key Tags	10		
Parka	1		
Raincoat	2		
Car Decals	2		
Miscellaneous			

SAMPLE 32
PERSONNEL FILE INDEX

Personnel File Index

Upon Hiring: Date:

Application received: _____

Applicant interviewed by _____ and on_____

Application approved: _____

Date hired: _____

TD-1 form completed: _____

Attorney General application form completed: _____

Fingerprint form issued: _____

Fingerprint form returned completed: _____

Uniform contract completed: _____

Recruit handbook issued: _____

Attorney General license received: _____

Company ID card issued: _____

Upon Termination:

Uniform returned: _____

Attorney General License returned: _____

Attorney General license forwarded to government: _____

Company ID card returned: _____

All documentation in file up to date: _____

File terminated: _____

Payroll file terminated: _____

EMPLOYEE TERMINATION REPORT

Employee Termination Report

TO BE COMPLETED BY THE EMPLOYER:

Name: _____   Date of Termination:_____

Please check the appropriate box: Voluntary termination [ ]

Fired [ ]

Lay-Off [ ]

Reason for termination: _____

_____

_____

_____

Comments on company/employee relations: _____

_____

_____

_____

COMPANY COMMENTS:

Uniform returned: Yes [ ]   No [ ]

License returned: Yes [ ]   No [ ]

Training book returned: Yes [ ]   No [ ]

Would employee be considered for rehire?   Yes [ ]   No [ ]

Where employee can be contacted in future: _____

_____

Employee appraisal: _____

_____

_____

Signature _____   _____
                                          Date

JOB DESCRIPTION FOR AREA SUPERVISOR

JOB DESCRIPTION FOR AREA SUPERVISOR

The Area Supervisor is accountable to the General Manager and is responsible for:

1. Enforcing conduct regulations and ensuring that all personnel perform duties as required. Good public relations, dress, and deportment are extremely important.

2. Ensuring that all security staff call in as required.

3. Ensuring that each guard is properly instructed and understands all security procedures.

4. Advising the General Manager of any deficiencies detected relating to personnel and/or property.

5. Ensuring that all decals issued to a site are posted in plain view at the site.

6. Must forward prior to the staff meeting the name of the person they select as guard of the month.

7. Must ensure that a high personal employee standard of deportment is maintained as per existing company policy.

8. Each guard is to be evaluated by the supervisor as per your list. These forms are to be left in a sealed envelope marked "Confidential" for the mobile patrol to pick up, or are to be brought in with the area supervisor to the meetings. If you are day shift, notify the main office of your request for a pick-up that night.

9. Discipline memos and verbal warnings are to be completed and forwarded immediately. Please refer to the Collective Agreement for complete understanding of procedures.

10. Reporting to the Office Manager daily.

11. Must be fully conversant with each of the returns required. Returns are all documentation required to be forwarded to the head office.

12. Assisting when required in the performance of guard duties in emergency situations.

13. Ensuring complete familiarity with the provision of the Local XXX Agreement.

14. Will not jeopardize the Company or its reputation by involvement with or direct participation in any organization deemed unacceptable by the Company President.

15. The efficient operation of all contracts within the assigned jurisdiction.

16. Promoting morale between the Company and its employees.

17. Supervising guard staff; attend sites during afternoon and graveyard shifts to inspect staff as required.

Additionally the supervisors were required to complete a Site Visit Log which was strictly an operational review (see Sample 35).

Based on our client arrangement and what probationary work system was in place we performed performance evaluation reports that would determine the probationary period was over and that overall site objectives were being met. This would also allow supervisors to put forward different employees as possible supervisors or for other promotions. See Sample 36.

In the download kit provided with this book there is also a summary sheet for performance appraisal records for your use.

6. Employee Discipline and Termination

Ensure you follow laws in your area regarding steps to discipline and terminate employees.

Establish a disciplinary procedure and a process that supervisors and operational staff have to follow.

Our situation required that we follow this step-by-step procedure:

1. Verbal warning (Sample 37).

2. Written warning (Sample 38).

3. Suspension.

4. Termination.

There were always exceptions based on the severity of the situation but we kept track of all matters on an employee discipline report.

7. Motivational Strategies: Promotions, Raises, Transfers

People like to be rewarded and not taken for granted. Often, security guards feel overlooked and undervalued. The truth is that this is often the case. In order to reduce turnover and maintain a positive company atmosphere, we set in place a variety of ways staff could be recognized.

One of our approaches was to allow an employee to request a promotion. He or she was required to fill out the form (see Sample 39) which would be evaluated.

Other times a supervisor or operations manager could request the promotion. It always allowed employees to seek opportunities within the company and not outside.

SITE VISIT LOG

Site Visit Log

Date: _____   Site: _____

Time: _____   Supervisor: _____

Guard(s) on Site: _____

Guard   Comments

Overall Appearance   _____
(uniform cleanliness, grooming, etc.)   _____
                                             _____

Job Knowledge   _____
(knowledge of post orders   _____
responsibilities)   _____

Overall Performance   _____
(interest, strengths, and weaknesses)   _____
                                             _____

Post Orders   _____
(condition, current)   _____

Equipment   _____
(condition, shortages)   _____
                                             _____

Site Logs & Reports   _____
(condition, content, etc.)   _____
                                             _____

Notebook   _____
(check format and condition)   _____
                                             _____

Other   _____
                                             _____
                                             _____

PERFORMANCE EVALUATION RECORD

Performance Evaluation Record

Employee: _____ Guard No. _____ Site: _____

Supervisor: _____

A. Not Observed   E. Fully Satisfactory
B. Marginal   F. Outstanding
C. Acceptable   G. Superior
D. Satisfactory

Category	Scale							Remarks
	A	B	C	D	E	F	G	
1. Knowledge of duties								
2. Support of supervisors								
3. Ability to produce accurate written work								
4. Appearance in uniform								
5. Acceptance of discipline								
6. Performance of duty								
7. Acts on his or her own initiative								
8. Ability to work without supervision								
9. Support of coworkers								
10. Support of subordinates								
11. Communication skills								
12. Familiar with company policy								
13. Response to emergency situation								
14. Punctuality								
15. Dependabilitty								

16. Is guard promotable to supervisor's position?   Yes [   ]   No [   ]

    Comments: _____

    _____

    _____

    _____

17. Additional remarks: _____

    _____

    _____

    _____

    Acknowledged by:

    Employee: _____   Date: _____

    Supervisor: _____   Date: _____

18. Comments of Operations Manager: _____

    _____

    _____

    _____

    Operations Manager: _____   Date: _____

19. Comments of President: _____

    _____

    _____

    _____

    Employee: _____   Date: _____

    President: _____   Date: _____

EMPLOYEE VERBAL WARNING NOTICE

Employee Verbal Warning Notice

Employee Name: _____   Date: _____

Position: _____   Location: _____

We wish to advise you of the following violation(s) of our Company Policy and Procedures that is/are inconsistent with your initial training and/or instruction.

In bringing the matter to your attention, we assure you that every assistance, including additional training where deemed necessary, will be given in order for you to attain the required standard.

A further review of your proficiency will be made and we will advise you accordingly.

You are hereby warned that any future instance of failing to adhere to our Company Policy and Procedures after the date of this warning could be considered as grounds for additional disciplinary action.

Violations, dates, and time: _____

_____

_____

_____

The above mentioned has been brought to my attention. I have received a copy of this document and I am aware that the original is to be retained in my personnel file.

Employee's comments: _____

_____

_____

_____

_____   _____
Employee's Signature   Date

_____   _____
Witness Signature   Position

1 Copy Personnel File

SAMPLE 38
EMPLOYEE DISCIPLINE REPORT

Employee Discipline Report

Name: _____   Job Title: _____

Employment Date: _____   Date Notice Given: _____

[ ] Warning   [ ] Suspension: Exact date of suspension _____ [ ] Termination

Previous Warnings (dates and nature of offense): _____

_____

_____

_____

_____

Current Infraction: _____

_____

_____

_____

Employee's Comments: _____

_____

_____

Additional Comments: _____

_____

_____

_____   _____
Employee's Signature   Supervisor's Signature

REQUEST FOR PROMOTION

Request for Promotion

Date: _____

Employee #: _____

Contract: _____

Present Rank: _____

Reason for Promotion: _____

_____

_____

Recommended for Promotion to: _____

_____

_____

Recommended by: _____

Reasons: _____

_____

_____

_____

_____

Effective Date: _____   Forms Forwarded   [ ] Yes

Salary Adjustment: _____   [ ] No

Approved: _____   Date: _____
       Field Supervisor

Approved: _____   Date: _____
       Operations Manager

Other things employees wanted that worked as incentives were a request for transfer, requests for days off over and above the regular days off, or an application for leave. All of the systems were structured and allowed for equitable treatment of employees. See the download kit for request forms for transfers, days off, and leave.

A bit of recognition goes a long way within companies. An effective strategy that we used was Employee of the Month. This is a well-known concept but one that recognizes achievement and rewards achievers accordingly. The individual would be recognized in the company newsletter and receive a trophy and gift certificate for dinner for two. Often, a short story would be written accompanying the announcement.

Involve your supervisors and management staff in recommending persons for monthly recognition. That way the whole company is involved. One year our guard dog won the Employee of the Month; he protected his mobile patrol driver when she was attacked.

We encouraged our clients to put forward employees for recognition as well. The information would be accumulated every month and personnel and operations would jointly make the selection of our employee of the month. There is a form for recommending employees in the download kit that came with this book.

There are other motivational strategies that you can explore and use. The key is to make it simple enough that it can be repeated, and not cumbersome so that no one wants to do the job of administering it.

Be inventive and positive. It will run through the company. Have clearly defined disciplinary procedures and motivational strategies. Consistent equitable treatment of employees will result in a successful company.

The download kit also includes other HR forms to help you as you build your company.

TRAINING

6

Trained staff is a key component to success in the security industry. Today, in times of terrorism and attacks on North American soil, it has become an even greater issue.

1. Employee Handbook

A good operational department will ensure that there is an Employee Handbook issued to every new hire either prior to or at the time of the person's orientation session. The handbook should cover a brief history of the organization so staff can represent their employer positively and answer questions knowledgeably; it also provides a sense of camaraderie amongst new hires; names and pictures of staff and the departments they are responsible for (this eliminates unnecessary calls); information on pay dates and how the pay will be provided (direct deposit; check; delivered to site); emergency numbers, and standard procedures for all staff. A sample manual is provided in the download kit (see the Sample Orientation Booklet).

2. In-house Orientation Sessions

A brief, motivational, orientation session for all new hires (four hours is plenty) assists in maintaining employee morale and encouraging new hires to feel part of the team. It will include many of the materials already discussed in the employee handbook and also provide a more personal sense that the people are important to the company, not just one of 100 or 1,000 employees. These sessions in a small company can be conducted by the owner and it provides employees with a sense of importance and validates their importance to the overall operational success of the company. Done properly, it can also help employees see how they can progress up the ladder in the company. Maintaining long-term loyal employees reduces financial losses at every level. The orientation session should provide plenty of motivation, explain motivational programs within the company, cover future opportunities and movement into supervision, and offer additional specialty training options (e.g., retail security, mobile patrol). A sample orientation/training session outline is provided in the download kit.

3. Site Orientations

On-site training is critical to understanding job expectations and client satisfaction. Additionally it prevents the inevitable complaints that management will receive over silly, site-specific things that should have been known.

4. Security Basics

That brings us to actual security training. Sadly this industry has been viewed as unprofessional for so long and the job of last resort for many that rebuilding the public perception will take time. The first step towards higher wages and higher charge-out rates is providing a trained personnel.

If you are fortunate to live in a state or province where minimum standards and legislated training is required, you are ahead of the game. This generally requires the potential security person to take, at his or her own cost, a minimum basic course. The courses generally cover the minimum a person has to know to accept keys, do a patrol, ask for identification, and the laws of his or her region.

British Columbia, as one example, makes security guard training prior to employment mandatory. This may not be case where you are located. If this is your situation, add another four-hour session on basics to security. This will save hours of your and your supervisors' time training people. Introduce a quiz at the end to ensure that people understand the basic concepts. This will definitely apprise management of potential staffing problems and can prevent job performance failure.

In the download kit you will find a sample of an Employee Orientation booklet.

If you do not have this requirement for employees, you can refer them to online courses that are now being made available by various Security Academies and/or develop your own. Developing your own course is not as cost-prohibitive as you may think. There are many manuals available that you can work with or you can purchase a training kit.

Regardless of which route you choose, you should ensure that the outline meets your needs; add to it or remove portions that do not apply. For example, in British Columbia, security guards do not carry weapons so there is no firearms training provided. You may, however, want to have a separate section on firearms and bring in a qualified trainer.

The same can be said for self-defense. Nobody is an expert after two hours of defense training but it can bring an awareness to them of what they need to improve.

REASONS SECURITY BUSINESSES FAIL (OR, WHAT TO AVOID)

7

Businesses fail for many reasons, but if you learn some of the possible reasons security businesses specifically may fail, hopefully you can avoid them in your venture. Some of this we've covered earlier in the book, but it all bears repeating.

1. What Are the Main Reasons Security Businesses Fail?

There are basically six reasons for the failure of a security company. They are: high staff turnover, client relations, servicing issues, job costing, training costs, and owner burnout.

1.1 Staff turnover

Staff turnover is one of the largest problems security companies face.

The industry is, generally, low paid and untrained. Some provinces in Canada have now set training standards that are mandatory for people going into the industry; BC requires that all guards take a basic course, at their own cost, prior to seeking employment. Some companies run their own internal training course. Whichever path you choose for training staff, you still need to provide motivation for your people. Most security jobs

involve either high levels of repetitive boring work or high-pressure conflict resolution.

To prevent turnover hire the right persons for the job. Ensure they are trained properly onsite and evaluated in a consistent manner. Provide them with a job description for a security guard as well as for the actual site. Prevent confusion! Involve the staff in feeling they are building your company and that they are proud of the company they work for. Management should make an effort to know their employees. Use motivation: Acknowledge birthdays, have employee of the month awards, celebrate outstanding achievement in the field, and make it a team!

If someone has a special skill use it and reward it. We had a security guard that was an exceptional artist and drew all of our Christmas cards! Celebrate your employees.

If you ignore the needs of the employees, you will increase your operations and scheduling costs as their time will be spent replacing no-show staff or staff quitting with no notice. This is a common problem in companies that do not have a link with their staff.

The foundation of a security company is the security guards. No guards = no work = no company.

1.2 Client relations

Years ago I was fortunate enough to obtain a contract with one of the largest hotel chains in the Lower Mainland. When I discussed with the client his reasons for the change he stated that in five years of the previous company providing a service he had never had a management or account rep attend his office to see how things were going. This is appalling client relations.

Do not take your client for granted. As you build your company it does become harder and harder to touch base with the smaller clients. But often the smaller clients are your referral base and sometimes the supporting base of your business. Set up a schedule for client visits to review how things are going. One suggestion I can provide is send out the Client Relations form with each invoice. Ask them to provide you with feedback. You can address a festering problem quickly by receiving this information. Also the client feels validated and acknowledged on a monthly basis.

I have never believed in the concept of "buying" your clients by taking them on fishing trips and such. Today more and more corporate clients are viewing that as conflicts of interest and have to be more concerned with their public image and privacy concerns. Good, solid, honest relationships with your client can build a strong business for you, provide security for your client, and prevent competition from succeeding in a takeover of the contract.

Good clients will refer others to you. Simultaneously, if they are not satisfied, it can set back your business.

1.3 Servicing issues

Monday mornings were always a nightmare in the security guard business. All the problems of the weekend, all the client concerns, and all the employee issues were front and center in operations. How do you prioritize and ensure all concerns are met? This is never an easy task.

First, sort the problems according to seriousness and contract value.

Second, assign and delegate conflict-resolution tasks to others in the office. If the office is you, then start with the list.

Third, deal with employee issues in priority order as well.

Servicing your clients is the key to maintaining contracts. This requires a prompt call to the clients (or email) advising them you are aware of the situation and what steps are going to be taken. Keep in touch with your clients. Even in the worst situation if your relationship is good, your company can probably survive the problem.

Have a form at your desk that identifies the problem and the resolution. Keep it in your client file for referral at the time of contractual renewal.

1.4 Job costing

The majority of start-up problems with security companies involve the pricing offered to obtain the contract. It serves no one to price your services too low. You have to be fully aware of what your cost of operating is, the net profit you want to make, and then the hourly wage you are paying or, if in a union, the wage you must pay. Are you offering benefits? All of this has to be costed properly.

The majority of businesses I have been brought in to help have simply not done this properly. The philosophy has always been that the cheapest bidder gets the job. This only works if you are a large company and can operate on volume net profit. Review your jobs and what they are costing you. If you are not making a decent return, either increase your price or walk away from the job. Do not keep jobs that are costing you money.

Refer to the guard costing form we covered in Chapter 2 and use it to decide on your hourly charge-out rates.

1.5 Training costs

Where guards must take a mandatory training course prior to employment part of the problem is solved, but on-site training is critical. On large sites with a lot of public interaction, having accurate information and public relations skills can present a good image of your company and reduce costs of guard replacement and client dissatisfaction.

There is never enough training. Guards need to have training that summarizes what the job actually is, and then training on the job, as well as upgrading as required.

When guards are not trained properly, their confidence on the job reduces and mistakes increase. When there are a lot of mistakes clients are unhappy. It is a circular problem and one that ties up management time.

This is an area that can become so costly that companies can no longer afford to operate. Refer again to Chapter 6 on training. Reduce site mistakes and make clients satisfied with trained staff.

1.6 Owner burnout

Many company owners find the security business, which operates 24 hours a day, seven days a week, one that can result in burnout. Most often burnout can be prevented by preparing properly; having your organizational skills in place; knowing and simplifying processes; using skilled and trained staff; knowing what a good job is; and not taking on every job.

If a company owner is jumping from problem to problem, eventually he or she will wear down. Smaller security companies require a lot of attention to succeed. Be prepared before you start.

CONCLUSION

When all is said and done, one of the most exciting industries to work in is the private security sector. Private security is required for every form of building — commercial, residential, retail centers, industrial, warehousing, marine sites, ski resorts — just name it. Services are available to individuals as well, from residential patrols, alarm systems, and access systems, to personal security and corporate risk issues.

In no other industry will you deal with all levels of executives and building structures. You will be providing safety and security advice and will use all your knowledge to help your clients.

It is challenging, fascinating, constantly changing, and it will keep you on your toes. There is never a dull moment in private security.

The easiest way to find success in the security industry is to be prepared and have a business and marketing plan in place; ensure your training and recruiting efforts will be successful; and that you have set up a stress-management program for yourself.

As you go on, stay on top of the industry; get certified; take professional development courses; and expand your business into new areas. This is an industry that is always growing.

Remember that your company is about you, your knowledge, and your staff's performance all coming together to keep your clients safe and happy.

DOWNLOAD KIT

Please enter the URL you see in the box below into your computer web browser to access and download the kit.

---

www.self-counsel.com/updates/securitybus/16kit.htm

The kit includes forms in PDF and MS Word formats. You can print and edit some of the forms to meet your needs:

- Business Plan Template
- Incident Report
- Monthly Inventory Report
- Billing Information
- — And more!

3/16